CUBA

HAITI

PUERTO
RICO

BRITISH
VIRGIN
ISLANDS

JAMAICA

DOMINICAN
REPUBLIC

US VIRGIN
ISLANDS

ANTIGUA

GUADELOUPE

CARIBBEAN SEA

DOMINICA

MARTINIQUE

ST LUCIA

ST VINCENT &
THE GRENADINES

BARBADOS

GRENADA

TRINIDAD
& TOBAGO

VENEZUELA

GUYANA

COLOMBIA

THE CURIOUS
BARTENDER'S
GUIDE TO
RUM

THE CURIOUS
BARTENDER'S
GUIDE TO
RUM

TRISTAN STEPHENSON

WITH PHOTOGRAPHY BY ADDIE CHINN
AND TRISTAN STEPHENSON

RYLAND PETERS & SMALL
LONDON • NEW YORK

Designers Geoff Borin, Paul Stradling
Commissioning Editor Nathan Joyce
Head of Production Patricia Harrington
Picture Manager Christina Borsi
Art Director Leslie Harrington
Editorial Director Julia Charles
Publisher Cindy Richards

Prop Stylist Sarianne Plaisant
Indexer Vanessa Bird

Originally published as *The Curious
Bartender's Rum Revolution* in 2017.
This abridged edition (with an expanded
Directory of Distilleries) published in
2020 by
Ryland Peters & Small
20–21 Jockey's Fields
London WC1R 4BW
and
341 E 116th St
New York NY 10029

www.rylandpeters.com

10 9 8 7 6 5 4 3 2 1

ISBN: 978-1-78879-238-7

A CIP record for this book is available from
the British Library.

US Library of Congress CIP data has been
applied for.

Printed in China

CONTENTS

INTRODUCTION

It was with equal parts of excitement and expectation that I embarked upon writing the original edition of this book, the fifth in the series, and by far the most ambitious. Why? Because this is rum, of course, the most diverse, contentious and fascinating of all the world's drinks… not to mention the most geographically dispersed!

As such, my journey has taken me across over 20 countries and dozens of islands. I've travelled to distilleries on horseback across active volcanoes, through rivers in a 4x4 and around tiny islets by boat. The lingering taste of rum has coated my mouth as I watched the sun set over the Amazon, and as the sun rose on the Virgin Islands. Rum made me dance the salsa in Cuba, drink all night with locals in Barbados and swim in the sea at dawn in Martinique. I've bought rum for $10 a gallon and $100 a shot. I've met people who depend on rum for the livelihood of their families, and have encountered islands that depend on rum for the livelihood of their communities. Is there another drink that offers such a taste of the human world?

Of course, this was never rum's intention. Rum is a spirit that has soaked into the history books and is bound to the places that make it. When we talk about *terroir* in wine and spirits, we refer to the impact of climate and geography on the taste of a drink. Rum's *terroir* is its past, and the flavour of many of the rums we drink today are an echo of island history more than they are the intentional formation of taste and aroma compounds. Rum does not need to be aged in cask to taste old – it is a multi-sensory mouthful of an era of discovery, conquest, colonization,

exploitation and trade.

But rum is more than just a quaint artefact of history's tectonic shifts. On many occasions, rum was there, making the history. Rum was the fire in the bellies of armies and navies, and the shackles that bound generations of slaves. It gave cause to revolutions: on plantations and across nations. It helped to establish global trade networks, kept the weak in bondage and turned rich men into gods.

In the 21st century, we are still living in the aftermath of the colonial era, and as rum struggles to find its place in the world, we need to remember these things more than ever. Rum is a rich tapestry of styles, and each island or national style is an intricate cultural pattern, described by tradition, technology and trade.

This means that rum style varies a lot. For better or for worse, "rum" is a loose category, vaguely strung around sugarcane and the 50-or-so countries that currently make it – bad news if you're looking for a neat summary; good news if you like being surprised and enjoy exploring new flavours.

I believe there's something for everyone in this spirit. Drunk neat, rum is a marvel. In mixed drinks, it is magical. Virtually any cocktail will willingly have its base spirit substituted for (the right) rum, but the stable of classics in this category speak for themselves: Daiquiri, Mojito, Piña Colada and Mai Tai to name but a few.

So let's go to the Caribbean and to some of the most beautiful places on earth. It won't always be pretty, though, as rum is far from a picture postcard. This is raw spirit – a spirit with real character. A free spirit, you might say.

HUMBLE ORIGINS

While it's likely – but by no means certain – that rum and sugarcane spirits originated in the Americas, the same cannot be said for the cane itself. Sugarcane, a fast- growing species of grass, is the base material from which all rums are made, whether it's in the form of the juice of the plant itself, the concentrated syrup made from the juice, or the molasses – the dark brown gloop that is leftover when you crystallize sugar out of the juice.

Over half of all the countries in the world grow sugarcane today, but 10,000 years ago you would have needed to travel to the island of New Guinea in the South Pacific to find any. We know that sugarcane is indigenous to the island, thanks to a unique ecosystem that exists there, of which sugarcane is a key component. Sugarcane is the sole source of food for the New Guinea cane weevil, a native species of beetle that bores into the cane stem and munches through the sweet fibrous interior. Also a resident of New Guinea is a type of tachinid fly that parasitizes the cane weevil with its larvae. The fly is dependent on the beetle for survival and the beetle is reliant on the sugarcane. For such a fruitful piece of symbiosis to have developed between the two insects, it is likely that sugarcane must have been growing on New

Guinea since the last ice age.

For early indigenous communities of New Guinea, known as the Papuans, the sugarcane offered an abundance of calories in the simplest possible form of energy: sugar. Early human settlers gnawed on the rough stem of cane, before developing tools to extract the juice, either with a couple of rocks, or with a pestle and mortar. The juice of the cane offered a nice, instant hit of energy, but the high sugar content that made it so desirable was also one of its major drawbacks. When combined with the tropical environment, the juice was prone to fermenting within a matter of days. The answer was to boil the juice down into a kind of honey, or to heat it until dark brown sugar crystals formed on the sides of the pan.

Of the hundreds of heirloom varieties of cane that grow wildly in New Guinea, only the sweetest, *Saccharum officinarum*, also known as Creole cane, was selected for cultivation. It was transported west to Indonesia, the Philippines and mainland Asia, and east to Fiji, Tonga, Hawaii and Easter Island.

Sugarcane was widely cultivated in India too, which was something Persian Emperor Darius I discovered when he invaded in 510 BC. When Alexander the Great arrived in India in 325 BC, one of his generals was in awe of the plant that

RIGHT It has been theorised that sugarcane was first domesticated as a crop in New Guinea around 6000 BC.

FAR RIGHT Sugarcane is still consumed by many modern-day Papuans, and for a few it forms a key component of their diet.

RIGHT Sugar was extremely rare in northern Europe until the 11th century, when Christian crusaders brought the sweet tasting spice back with them from the Holy Lands.

BELOW RIGHT The earliest types of commercial Indian sugar mills were effectively giant garlic presses. The extracted juice flowed out of the crucible into a receiving vessel.

could "bring forth honey without the help of bees, from which an intoxicating drink can be made." Later, around the second century AD, the first recorded sugar mill was built in India and scholars documented how to manage a cane plantation. Sugarcane infiltrated Indian society on many levels; it was used medicinally for humans and as food for elephants, and the juice was fermented into wine known as *gaudi* or *sidhu*. It also became a symbol used in Hindu and Buddhist faiths. It's also India that we must thank for the word "sugar", which is thought to be derived from the Prakrit word *sakkara*, meaning sand or gravel.

SUGAR ARRIVES IN EUROPE

Having conquered India and infiltrated China and Japan, in around 600 AD, cane was transported west, to Persia. The timing was exquisite, as the rise of the Islamic faith would soon serve as a vehicle for sugar's journey further westward to Europe.

The Arabs were a well-organised and technologically impressive bunch. The vast scale of their rapidly growing empire

meant that trade between regions was fluid. Their agricultural prowess and advanced water management systems allowed plantations to flourish like never before. By the turn of the eighth century AD, the Umayyad Empire stretched from Pakistan to Portugal and all along the north of Africa. Sugarcane was grown on the banks of the River Nile, and was cultivated by the Moors on Sicily, Malta and southern Spain. The island of Cyprus became a vivid green Arab sugar garden. One Italian traveller wrote of Cyprus in the 15th century that "the abundance of the sugarcane and its magnificence are beyond words."

Arabic physicians used sugar in a variety of medicinal preparations, such as *shurba* (sherbet), which back then was sweet hot water taken as medicine; *rubb*, a preserve of fruits in sugar; and *gulab*, a rose-scented sweet tea.

Those who were committed to the Islamic faith abstained from drinking, so fermented cane juice was off the table. There is no evidence that the Arabs or the Moors ever distilled fermented cane products either, but given that it was the Moors, who introduced distillation to Europe by way of Italy, and considering the freedom of access to sugar products that these people enjoyed, I don't think it's too much of a stretch to speculate that the experiments of an Islamic alchemist might have resulted in the world's first proto-rum.

Northern Europe would have to wait until the Crusades before they got their first real taste of sugar. Crusaders brought sugar back to England from the Holy Lands, and by 1243 the Royal Household of Edward I was getting through nearly 3,000 kg (6,600 lbs) of sugar in a single year. At that time in Europe, sugar was regarded as a spice, valued as highly as vanilla or saffron today. A 1-kg (2.2-lbs) bag of sugar would have set you back the equivalent of £100 ($125) in today's money. Reserved only for those with sufficiently deep pockets, sugar was used by the wealthy as an extravagant signifier of status, added even to savoury dishes just because, well… why not? The hunger for sweetness was not limited to the upper classes, though. The compulsion for sugar was universal, and the human brain was wired to want it.

As European powers clambered to reclaim lands from the Moors, they discovered areas dedicated to growing sugarcane. Learning the secrets of cane cultivation, they planted more wherever it would grow. But besides the most southerly islands, Europe was not particularly well suited to growing sugarcane. Winters were too cold and the rainfall was insufficient. Rhodes, Crete, Cyprus, and Malta operated plantations under Christian rule, and the cane was shipped to Venice for refinement into sugar.

The early 15th century saw Portugal conducting increasingly adventurous voyages along the west coast of Africa. In 1421 the island of Madeira was sighted by sailors passing by the west coast of Morocco. This island, which would prove to be a vital step (both physically and commercially) toward the colonial plantation system, was very well suited to sugarcane cultivation. The first shipments of sugar arrived in Bristol, England in 1456, and 50 years later, Madeira was producing 1,800 tons (2,015 US tons) of sugar a year: equivalent to around half of all the sugar consumed in Europe at that time.

Another crucial development in the story of sugar and of rum occurred at around the same time. In 1444 the first boatload of 235 slaves was shipped out of Lagos by the Portuguese. A cheap workforce would prove to be an essential component of plantation economics, and these were the first of millions of African slaves whose lives would be lost to sugar.

NEW WORLD ORDER

Christopher Columbus's historic first voyage of 1492, after securing the support of King Ferdinand and Queen Isabella of Spain, was intended to plot new trade routes with the East Indies. The Spanish had been slower at entering the spice and silk trade than the Dutch or English, owing to the protracted Reconquista of the Iberian peninsular from its Muslim occupants.

Columbus proposed a radical shortcut

to the east (by heading to the west) and with it presented the opportunity to gain a competitive edge over rival European powers in the hunt for gold, silk, pepper, cloves and ginger.

On the first voyage, the trade winds propelled the navigator across the Atlantic in five weeks, first sighting land at San Salvador in the Bahamas (which Columbus was convinced was Japan), then Cuba (which he thought was China) and then Hispaniola. The island of Hispaniola – now shared between Haiti and the Dominican Republic – was of particular interest to Columbus because he believed a wealth of gold lay hidden there. He encountered the friendly indigenous Taíno people and wrote about them in his letters to King Ferdinand and Queen Isabella. Columbus received small gifts of gold and pearls from the Taíno, and even left a party of 39 men behind to establish a small colony.

Upon his return to Spain, Columbus was welcomed as a hero. He presented the Spanish monarchs with tobacco, pineapples, a turkey, and a hammock, all of which were previously unknown to European culture. On his second voyage

ABOVE "I know you've been getting along fine without us Europeans, but it's time for a change around here. Now – tell me where the gold is".

in 1493 Columbus returned to Hispaniola, this time with a fleet of 17 ships, 1,200 men and 1,500 sugarcane shoots.

Many history books include accounts of Columbus and his son Ferdinand, who oversaw the planting of sugarcane on Hispaniola on the second voyage. Columbus's father-in-law was a sugar planter on Madeira and Columbus was no doubt aware of the crop's value in Europe. He was a man driven by greed as much as he was adventure, and in the back of his mind was a promise from the Spanish crown of a 10% share of all profits generated by newly established

LEFT The method for making sugar in the Caribbean remained almost unchanged for over three centuries.

colonies. But according to Fernando Campoamor in his landmark 1985 book *El Hijo Alegre de la Cana de Azúcar*, the explorer was unable to conduct the cultivation experiments he intended because the delicate plants did not survive the sea crossing. What is certain is that seven years later, in 1500, Pedro di Atienza successfully transported and planted sugarcane seedlings on Hispaniola. It was probably only then that the early settlers discovered that sugarcane flourished in the tropical Caribbean climate.

Gold, on the other hand, remained elusive. So too did the promised spices and silk. These lands were not the East Indies after all, although the likes of Christopher Columbus would go to their death beds still believing it so. The absence of any immediate value is one of the reasons that the Spanish defended the Caribbean so poorly over the 100 years that followed, instead directing their attentions to the precious metals that Central America offered. This allowed the Dutch, English and French to swoop in and pick up their share of the island booty. The Europeans realised the potential of sugarcane. Consequently, the plantation system and the sugar-refining industry, rather than the harvesting of spices and silk production, were destined to shape the economy and society of the West Indies and Brazil.

As the sea spray settled on the shores of the Caribbean region, it must have seemed a place of enormous agricultural potential to the European settlers: fertile lands, clear waters, year-round sunshine, and a trusting native populace just waiting to be put to task – there was a problem with that, however.

Within the space of a single generation the indigenous Carib, Warao and Arawak people who occupied most

of the Caribbean islands were almost entirely eradicated. As colonies expanded, tens of thousands melted away panning for gold in rivers, in fruitless mining operations, or on plantations, and those who resisted slavery were slaughtered by European forces (mostly Spanish) who possessed superior weaponry and a greater knowledge of how to use it. Many, it seems were executed under orders from Christopher Columbus himself. The biggest killer of all, however, was disease. Measles, mumps and smallpox plagued the indigenous populace, who lacked the antibodies and medicine to combat European viruses effectively. The Dominican Friar Bartolomé de las Casas wrote that when he arrived in Hispaniola in 1508, "there were 60,000 people living on this island, including the Indians; so that from 1494 to 1508, over three million people had perished from war, slavery and the mines." He added: "Who in future generations will believe this?"

FAST-GROWING GRASS

In the early 1500s, the Portuguese established the first sugar plantations in South America. They were in the states of Bahia and Pernambuco, on Brazil's moist eastern coastline. The grass flourished, and by 1550 there were five sugar refineries in Brazil, and the

Portuguese were shipping sugarcane presses and vats over from Europe to aid the pursuit. But compared to other tropical commodities, like cotton or tobacco, sugarcane was a much tougher beast to manage. A sugar planter needed a superior understanding of agricultural practices, factory management skills, the ability to deal with agricultural diseases, a huge supply of water and enough money to bankroll the whole operation as lands were cleared and crops planted. But more than anything, a planter needed a cheap and plentiful labour force. Brazilian natives were hunted down for this purpose in expeditions called *bandeiras*. Once captured, these men and women were put to task, but as was the case in Hispaniola, they quickly succumbed to diseases. A bigger, more dependable workforce was needed, and fortunately for Portugal, they had access to one.

The West African slave trade had been held in state of near monopoly by the Portuguese since the 1440s, so the next logical step was to connect the dots between their trading outpost in Elmina (on Africa's Gold Coast) and their developing colonies in the Americas. That "Middle Passage", as it is known, was sailed for the first time by Portuguese mariners in 1510. These sailors brought black slaves with them and recorded their presence on the ship's manifest. Thousands more slaves followed over the next 378 years.

The "first in, last out" approach was a consistent theme in the history of slavery. Cuba, Hispaniola and Puerto Rico were all early adopters of African slaves and among the most reluctant to give it up (some would argue that the Dominican Republic still hasn't – see pages 91–92) and they too required the manpower to manage their extensive sugarcane

TOP Despite being the largest Caribbean island, the scale of sugar production on Cuba didn't truly ramp up until the late 19th century.

ABOVE In Brazil, on the other hand, large-scale sugar production was relentless from the late 16th century onwards.

plantations. Spain's obsession with gold had spread their empire thinly across the Central American belt. With the Spanish weakened by the endeavour, the British, Dutch and French made it their business to harass both their ships and settlements persistently through the unofficial employment of *bucaneros* and privateers (see pages 23–24). Naturally the mercantilist Spanish were none too keen for their colonies to trade with rival nations, and these embargoes stunted the growth of the Spanish sugarcane industry to the point where the crop didn't become dominant on any of their occupied islands until the 19th century.

Back to the 17th century, and sugar production in Brazil was showing no signs of abating. This was partly thanks to the Dutch West India Company, which had seized the colonial territory of Pernambuco from the Portuguese in 1630 and began rampantly planting more cane. Ten years later, the Dutch began shipping slaves from equatorial Africa, which became a critical juncture in the establishment of further Dutch plantations, as well as securing sugar's position in the infamous triangular trade (see pages 20–21). In 1612, the total production of sugar in Brazil had reached 14,000 tons (15,400 US tons). But by the 1640s, Pernambuco alone had 350 refineries, exporting more than 24,000 tons (26,500 US tons) of sugar annually to Amsterdam.

Sugar was becoming difficult to ignore as a New World commodity as demand for sugar in Europe continued to rise. It was around this time that the British and French Caribbean took a greater interest in sugarcane cultivation. The British established a settlement on Barbados in 1627 and the French followed suit on Martinique in 1635. The first plantations on these islands were used to grow cotton and tobacco, or fustic wood and indigo (both used in the manufacturing of dyes). Early settlers persevered with these crops for the better part of two centuries, but in the 1640s, there was a rapid shift towards sugarcane. This came about after the Portuguese recaptured Pernambuco from the Dutch West India Company, who immediately sought to establish trading opportunities in the Caribbean.

And so it was that Dutch traders sailed north. Spilling into the Caribbean, they presented the English and French a complete commercial and logistical solution for sugarcane, along with a century's worth of combined practical know-how of how to run a plantation. The seed was planted, and once established the sugar production in the Caribbean increased at a furious rate. Barbados's sugarcane production grew from 7,000 (7,700 US tons) to 12,000 tons (13,200 US tons) in the second half of the 17th century, while on Guadeloupe, exports grew from 2,000 tons (2,200 US tons) in 1674 to 10,000 tons (11,000 US tons) in the space of 25 years.

Over the next 100 years, sugar would become the most valuable trading commodity in the world; it became very much the oil of its day. But more than just a commodity, sugar production provided one of the original means and motivations for European expansion, colonization and control in the New World, precipitating a course of events that would forever shape the destiny of the Western Hemisphere.

RUM'S SLOW BIRTH

By the middle of the 17th century, sugar was being grown on most of the islands of the Caribbean, and it was during this period that the first British and French rums were distilled. Exactly where and when this happened is a matter that we shall debate shortly, but one thing that we can be sure of is that rum was not the first alcoholic beverage enjoyed by New World booze hounds.

Richard Ligon, an English colonist who lived in Barbados between 1647 and 1650, gives us one of the best insights about life on the island during its early English colonization. In his book *A True and Exact History of the Island of Barbados*, he wrote, "The first [drink], and that which is most used in the Island, is Mobbie, a drink made of potatoes." Mobbie was a kind of potato beer, produced using a variety of fermented red (sweet) potatoes known to the native Caribs as *mâ'bi*. It was the job of the women to boil the potatoes and mash them up, then add them to large earthenware vessels along with water, molasses and spices, such as ginger. The mixture would then naturally ferment over a period of a few days and your efforts would be rewarded with a kind of spiced potato beer.

Similar drinks to this were made from the crop cassava. Known as *oüicou* in the Carib language, in Barbados cassava wine was called *parranow* or *perino*. According to Ligon, its taste was comparable to "the finest English beer". Many Carib women wound up toothless after a lifetime's *oüicou*-making, which involved chewing on a mouthful of grated cassava, then spitting it into a calabash (a container formed from the shell of a gourd-like fruit) filled with water and more cassava. The enzymes in the women's saliva converted the starches into fermentable sugars and airborne yeast took care of alcohol production. The acid in the raw cassava was responsible for the tooth decay.

Other wines and beers were enjoyed too, produced from the fermentation of plantain, bananas, plums, oranges, limes, wild grapes and tamarind. Pineapple wine – which even on paper sounds delicious – got a thumbs up from Ligon, with the ever-enthusiastic colonist describing it as "the Nectar which the Gods drunk". The French missionary Père Labat also remarked on the "extremely agreeable" taste of pineapple wine.

Delicious as some of these drinks may have been, there is no evidence to suggest that any of them were ever

ABOVE A 17th-century woodcut print depicts the "personal involvement" of manufacturing cassava wine on the Caribbean island of Hispaniola.

distilled into strong spirits, and there's a very good reason for that. At the turn of the 17th century, distillation in Europe was seldom practised by anyone other than physicians who were generally trying to uncover the next big medicinal cure-all or the secret to eternal life. But strong alcohol was about to enter a transitional phase that would see it graduate from the medicine cabinet to the bar room.

Distillation was introduced to Europe by the Moors in the 11th century – yes, the same people that brought sugarcane to the Europeans' attention – after which it was documented by scholars at the earliest recorded medical school in Salerno, southern Italy, before migrating north to Antwerp, Amsterdam, and other places that didn't necessarily start with an 'A'. The precursor to whisky, *aqua vitae* ("water of life"), had found its way to Ireland and Scotland by the middle of the 15th century, where it was renamed in the Gaelic language *uisge beatha*. Meanwhile, the Dutch, who were among the earliest practitioners of distillation in Europe, were experimenting with *brandewijn* ("burnt wine"): a grape-based spirit that would later be known as "brandy".

Critical to a distillation operation was the still itself, which would heat the fermented beer or wine, evaporating the alcohol (which has a lower boiling point than water) and condense it into a crystal clear concentrate. In Europe, the first commercial distilleries were purpose-built to manufacture genever, whisky and brandy. In the Caribbean, they came about as supplementary operations to a sugar refinery. The oldest pot stills were generally under 450 litres (100 US gallons) in size and made from hammered copper. Brazil was ground zero for distillation in the Americas, probably receiving stills by way of Madeira, and it was most likely sugarcane that was used as the base material for their experiments. In 1533, when sugar mills were established at São Jorge dos Erasmos, Madre de Deus, and São João, the planters also installed copper alembic stills to produce *aguardiente de caña* ("fire water of cane"), which is the earliest example of the spirit that would later be known as *cachaça*. The ruins of Brazil's first *cachaça* distillery at São Jorge dos

Erasmos have been excavated recently by archaeologists and designated as a historical site. In fact, the uptake of distillation in Brazil was so frenzied that, according to some historical accounts, Brazil had 192 distilleries in 1585, and that number was set to double by 1630.

For close to 100 years, Brazil remained the only place in the Americas producing cane spirits. As inconceivable as this may seem, it's a solid depiction of the extreme isolation that the earliest New World colonies experienced, and the poor exchange of knowledge that came as a result. This was the dawn of globalization, but it was also a time where journeys took weeks not hours and the dissemination of knowledge took decades.

The British and French had a fairly good excuse of course – they weren't farming sugarcane during this period – but the Spanish? The Spanish Empire were operating sizeable sugarcane plantations in Mexico, Cuba, Puerto Rico and Hispaniola, as far back as the 1550s. There's no record of distillation in any Spanish colonies until the 1640s, however, which more than anything is

LEFT Unlike this large 19th-century distillery, the first Caribbean rum plants were merely addenda to sugar mills.

indicative of the Spanish Empire's isolationist approach to global domination.

The rise of Caribbean rum ultimately came as a result of that most dependable of all ocean trading people, the Dutch. Holland dominated international commerce in the 17th century – their East and West Indies Trading Corporations arguably became the world's first mega corporations. This was a nation that wasn't motivated by discovering gold, or by a desire to convert the godless natives to Christianity. The Dutch were capitalists, driven by the commercial opportunity and saleable commodities like coffee, spices and sugarcane. Sugar's exit route from Brazil came via the Dutch, who, when forced to relinquish Dutch Brazil in the 1640s (see page 15), required immediate action to keep their sugar empire running. It would be the Dutch who would later supply most of the copper stills in the Caribbean, too.

In 1644, a Dutchman by the name of Benjamin Da Costa brought sugar refining equipment to Martinique and it's possible that he brought alembic stills with him too. It's also possible that they were already there, as a manuscript from 1640 (when the colony was only five years old) states that the slaves were drinking a "strong eau de vie that they call brusle ventre [stomach burner]." Since it's unlikely that slaves would have access to imported brandy, one would have to assume that this *brusle ventre* was distilled from a locally grown source of fermentable sugar – and yes, it was probably sugarcane.

In Barbados, however, it seems that distillation might have preceded the full-scale arrival of sugarcane to the island. Sir Henry Colt, a British traveller, visited the four-year-old colony of Barbados in 1631, when there were scarcely more than a few hundred inhabitants on the island. Colt reported that the people were "devourers upp of hott [sic] waters and such good distillers thereof." Whether these spirits were made from cane or some other vegetable or fruit remains a mystery, but five years later, the Dutch émigré Pietr Blower brought distillery equipment to Barbados from Brazil. This was a crucial step in the development of rum, as it is alleged that

Blower was the man who introduced the concept of distilling spirits from waste from the sugar-refining process, rather than valuable cane juice.

For centuries, sugar refineries had been converting sugarcane juice into sweet crystals, but nobody had found a good use for the molasses – the thick, dark syrup that was left behind. Up to 40% of the weight of the molasses was pure sugar, but the technical practicalities and associated costs of extracting the remaining sugar meant that it wasn't worth the effort. Like a tightly locked chest containing a wealth of sweet treasure, as long as the chest remained locked, it was worthless. For many islands, molasses was deemed too bulky and not cost-effective to ship abroad.

In some cases it was simply discarded into the ocean – enough to "make a province rich" according to one Hispaniola official in 1535 – or used as a fertilizer for the next season's sugarcane crops. Sometimes it was used as animal feed, or reboiled to make a cheaper form of sweetener known as *peneles*, which was used to make gingerbread. In most instances it contributed to the diets of slaves, whether as food itself, or as a fermented drink. The tropical climate, coupled with high levels of sugar in the molasses, meant that fermentation was inevitable – especially given that molasses was commonly left lying around for weeks at a time. The consumption of fermented molasses was not limited only to slaves, either. Colonial life was tough on everyone, and alcohol an essential distraction to the hardships of the age of discovery. In a part of the world where beer, wine and spirits were all imported at great expense, one couldn't be too discriminating over the source of the intoxicant.

One of the earliest references of

ABOVE This map of Barbados was drawn in 1683, by which time the British had already controlled the island for over 55 years.

colonists consuming molasses wine comes from 1596 when English chaplain Dr Layfield reported that the Spanish colonies in Puerto Rico enjoyed a drink called guacapo, which was, "made of Molasses (that is, the coarsest of their Sugar) and some Spices". This molasses wine was known as *guarapo* and *guarapa* to the Spanish, *garapa* to the Portuguese (in Brazil) and *grappe* to the French.

KILL DEVIL

Once sugarcane spirit becoming a regular feature in the plantations of the New World, it was only right that they were given a proper name. It should have been a simple affair, but this was booze birthed out of effluent made by slaves – it was never going to be an easy process. Sadly, history is not so complete that all the colloquial terms and slang references to this spirit that would later be known as rum are available to us. The road to a liquor called "rum" was no easier than any of the rest of rum's turbulent passage through time. What we do know is that before rum there was "kill devil".

Why the spirit was called kill devil is not clear. Probably because it was strong – perhaps strong enough to kill a devil? – but more likely through a corruption of language of one sort or another. The French referred to the stuff as *guildive*, which is probably a compound of the old French word *guiller* (meaning "fermentation") or the Malay word *giler* ("crazy") and *diable* ("devil"). When the English heard it spoken they distorted into the suitably dangerous sounding kill devil.

Kill Devil bears no resemblance to "rum", of course. "Rum" is cited by most historians as an abbreviation of "rumbullion": a word originating from the county of Devon, England, meaning "a great tumult or uproar" and may have been used by Devonian settlers in Barbados. Rumbullion was first mentioned in 1652 by Barbados resident and wealthy sugar planter Giles Silvester, and it's the only time we see the word linked with kill devil. He was clearly not a fan of rumbullion: "the chiefe fuddling they make in the island is Rumbullion, alias Kill-Devil, and this made of suggar [sic] canes distilled, a hot, hellish, and terrible liquor."

For me, a more likely scenario than the borrowing of a faintly appropriate Devonian word, is that rumbullion came about as a fusion of different English and French words. In 16th-century England, the word "rum" was used to mean "excellent, fine or good" and was informally coupled with "booze" to form the Elizabethan slang term "rum booze", which was used colloquially to reference wine (though appearing very little in texts). John P. Hughes, a linguistics expert and the author of *The Science of Language* suggests that at the time, "rum booze" was popularly pluralized into the word "rumboes", which, in turn was singularised into "rumbo" to refer to "strong punch". Rum was simply a shortened form of "rumbo". The word rumbullion may have emerged from the amalgamation of rum and the French word *bouillon* (meaning "hot drink"), referring to a hot, strong, punch. If this is beginning to sound confusing, we're not quite done yet.

There are other competing theories about the origin of the word rumbullion, however. Some historians suggest that rumbullion derives from the large drinking glasses used by Dutch seamen known as a *roemer*. Others think that rum could also be derived from the word *aroma* or the latter part of the Latin word for sugar: *saccharum*. Some researchers have posited that the word rum heralds from the Sanskrit *roma* ("water"), an opinion shared by many 19th-century dictionaries. Other etymologists have mentioned the Romani word "rum", meaning "strong" or "potent". However the word "rum" came about, it was also the basis of "ramboozle" and "rumfustian", both popular British drinks in the mid-17th century. Neither was made with rum, however, but rather eggs, ale, wine, sugar and various spices.

The first recorded use of the word "rum" to describe a sugarcane spirit comes from 1650, and it also comes from the island of Barbados. A deed for the sale of the Three Houses Plantation in the parish of St Philip, Barbados included in its inventory "four large mastick cisterns for liquor of rum." Further confirmation that rum was here

to stay (and indeed that it was on the move) comes from English traveller George Warren's 1667 book *An impartial description of Surinam upon the continent of Guiana in America*: "Rum is a spirit extracted from the juice… called Kill-Devil in New England!"

This blunt, monosyllabic word seemed a fitting sound to describe a drink of such humble origins. "Rum" was quickly adopted by planters in the Spanish- and French-speaking colonies of the Caribbean, translating to *rhum* and *ron* respectively.

THE TRIANGULAR TRADE

Triangular trade is the name given to a trading system conducted between three specific areas. The best-known triangular trade route was the commercial platform that linked the Caribbean and American colonies with their European colonial powers and the west coast of Africa between the 16th and 19th centuries. This trading system was necessary because of the regional demand for the goods generated by the other regions in the triangle, and was propelled by the powerful trade winds that traversed the Atlantic – for an African slave it must have seemed that even the planet itself was aligned against them.

In the Caribbean, ships were loaded with sugar, rum, coffee and spices, which were sent to Europe where the ship's captain traded for manufactured items, such as textiles, cutlery and weapons. Leaving Europe, the ships next sailed south to Africa, where they traded for human cargo. The slaves were transported across the Atlantic Ocean to the Caribbean, where they were sold at auction and sent to work on the plantations, growing sugar and ensuring the continuation of the cycle. As the colonies of North America became better established, a second triangular trading system was developed that effectively cut Europe out of the equation. Both systems are paramount to the history of sugar and rum because an estimated two-thirds of the 1.5 million African slaves who made the voyage between 1627 and 1775 were put to work on sugarcane plantations.

Although the slave trade was abused to its fullest and most abominable extent by European powers during the 17th and 18th centuries, the African slave trade existed in Africa and the East Indies as far back as the 1100s. Operated by the kings of West Africa, tribesmen from Central and South African regions were kidnapped and sold by chiefs from Angola and the Ivory Coast, often in exchange for *akpeteshie* or *burukutu* – a type of date palm wine.

This fondness for fermented alcoholic beverages among the kings of Africa was important, as along with cloth, gunpowder and ironware, it would later be leveraged by European traders keen to exchange rum for slaves. Distilled spirits were unknown in Africa, so when these supercharged liquids called *rum*, *rhum, aguardiente* and *cachaça* were offered to the kings, they were keenly received. Whether it was rum or some other manufactured commodity from Europe or the colonies, this exchange of product for human cargo is cited by some historians as the birth of capitalism and the global economy.

During the six-week voyage across the ocean, on average one-third of all slaves perished en route. Those that didn't die were often malnourished, ill and/or psychologically traumatized. Traders recognized this, so they compensated for their lost human cargo by overcrowding their ships, which really only had the effect of worsening the problem. The slaves were chained into the hold so tightly that there was no room to move. Men were afforded a space of 180 x 37 cm (6 x 1¼ ft), and women even less. Water and food were heavily rationed, and buckets provided the only means of disposing of human waste. The gruesome living conditions lead to outbreaks of typhoid, measles and yellow fever. In some extreme instances, 90% of a ship's hold were pronounced dead upon arrival in port. On some occasions, entire ships were lost, as slaves mounted insurrections against their captors. Some of these mutinies were successful, such as the *Clare* in 1729, and others resulted in the death of everybody on board.

The crew, which generally comprised lowlifes and criminals, really didn't have it much better. They were just as vulnerable to contracting diseases, but also bound to the backbreaking tasks that filled their days and weeks.

GREAT RUMBLINGS

Despite the availability of molasses, the earliest rums were often made from the sucrose-rich skimmings or scum that

ABOVE Slave ships varied in size and capacity, but the larger models could transport up to 200 slaves, albeit in wretched conditions, in a single voyage.

were collected during the sugar refining process. Now this stuff really was useless, and the collection and subsequent fermentation of the skimmings illustrates, more than anything, the thriftiness of the early sugarcane planters. There are reports of distilleries in both the French and British Caribbean making rum in this way through the 1640s, until molasses finally became the *de facto* base material across all Caribbean islands.

As is the case with most things in rum's history, this came about as a result of economics more than good taste. Most plantations in the mid-1600s made two types of sugar: dark muscovado, and low-quality peneles. This approach resulted in the maximum quantity of sugar with as little as possible waste, which, in turn, limited the quantity of rum that could be manufactured. Semi-refined white sugar sold for twice the price of muscovado, but it also generated more waste. As the demand for rum increased, planters on every island in the Caribbean turned to molasses.

The earliest account of rum-making in Barbados comes from Richard Ligon's *A True and Exact History of Barbados* (1647). Ligon offers detailed drawings of a sugar mill and still-house, which comprised two pots and a cistern. The cistern was likely made from mastic wood (in a time when the forest of Barbados were still being cleared) and was presumably used for fermenting the sugar skimmings from the mill. The pots differ in size, suggesting a similar routine to that which is used in the production of malt whisky, where the larger of the two pots was used for the principal distillation of "low wines", and the smaller used for the second distillation of high-strength spirit. This is a surprisingly sophisticated setup for the 17th century, and far more elaborate than the stills being employed on Martinique during the same period.

Jean-Baptiste du Tertre, who toured Martinique in the 1640s, describes in his 1654 book *Histoire Générale des îles Saint-Christophe, de la Guadeloupe, de la Martinique et autres de l'Amérique* a single pot-still that he calls a *vinaigrerie*. It is connected to a worm-tub condenser and is operated by slaves, who made an "intoxicating liquor" using sugar skimmings for personal consumption.

Over the 50 years that followed rum's uneasy birth, the spirit swept across the Caribbean like a tropical typhoon. What had, at first, been a drink for slaves, was now starting to fill the punch bowls of white planters, but this wasn't all that it was filling – rum soon took its rightful place aboard ship's manifest, stored in barrels and stacked in the cargo hold of every trading ship across the region.

The steep rise in rum consumption through the Caribbean and later in Europe meant that rum needed to get its game face on. The 17th century would see rum reinvent itself time after time, evolving from skimmings-based

RIGHT This 1823 drawing forms part of the series "Ten Views in the Island of Antigua" and shows slaves loading barrels of sugar onto boats.

moonshine to a fully fledged industry that would make fortunes for the planters in Barbados, Jamaica and Sainte-Domingue.

Speaking of Barbados, the esteemed distiller William Y-Worth wrote an account of a Barbadian rum recipe in 1707 in which the product was fermented "together with the remains of the former distillation". This is the first reference to the use of "dunder" (the residual liquid after distilling rum) in rum production. It's interesting that the recipe does not herald from Jamaica, where the practice would become a hallmark of the Jamaican style (see page 60).

Samuel Martin, an Irish immigrant with plantations in Antigua, operated an estate that covered 245 hectares (605 acres), of which 160 hectares (400 acres) was used for growing cane in 1756. Martin published "An Essay on Plantership" in 1786 that includes a recipe for rum comprising, "one-third scum from cane juice, one-third of water from washing the coppers, and one-third lees." This was left to ferment for 24 hours, after which molasses is added gradually to build up the yeast cell count and "yield a due proportion of rum".

With more plantation operators recording their recipes, further refinement and specialization ensued. The late 18th century is full of accounts from experienced distillers (especially in Jamaica) who were, for the first time, aware of *terroir*, the importance of pH in fermentation, consistency and more refined distillation techniques. Rum had well and truly evolved beyond the second-thought hooch to an art that required careful consideration and documentation. Why? Because it made money, of course.

RUMMING AROUND THE BRITISH ISLES

The 18th century was a period of massive growth for the Caribbean rum industry, which saw exports to Britain, North America and parts of Northern Europe increase at an astonishing rate. In 1690, little if any rum was imported into the UK. In 1697, a measly 100 litres (26 US gallons) or one-quarter of a sherry barrel arrived on British shores. By 1750, 4.5 million litres (1.2 million US gallons) of rum arrived in British ports, and that number was set to triple over the next two decades to the point where rum accounted for 25% of all the spirits consumed in British Isles in 1780.

The sheer volume of rum available to the British drinker didn't do much to elevate the spirit's reputation, and for the time being it occupied a curious position in the eyes of the 18th-century drinker. This was a spirit that was labelled by its challengers as a drink for slaves or common men, and yet it was being manufactured by wealthy plantation owners with strong connections to the British aristocracy. As such, the upper classes, whose focus remained fixated on wine and brandy, saw rum as a quaint, yet potentially dangerous and exotic novelty. The lower classes stuck with the "bang for your buck" mantra, which, in London at least, meant gin – 45 million litres (12 million US gallons) of it in 1750 alone. That just left the middle classes, who were priced out of the brandy market and keen to avoid genever so as to disassociate themselves from the gin-guzzling masses.

But this was more than just a case of class and financial resources. Availability played a big part in the decision-making process, too, and nowhere more so than in the lesser populated extremities of the

British Isles, especially towns and cities on the western coastline, like Bristol, Liverpool and Falmouth, which developed into industrial trading hubs for Caribbean imports. The availability of rum in these towns lead to some entrepreneurial types establishing blending houses. Amazingly, there are accounts of sugar refineries and distilleries opening in Glasgow, Liverpool and London, as far back as the 1670s. Given that so little (if any) rum was imported into Britain at that time, it's quite possible that the first taste of rum for many British people was in fact British rum!

As volumes grew through the latter part of the 1700s, one thing remained fairly steady: around 85% of the rum imported was Jamaican, and most of the remaining 15% was from Barbados, who at the time exported more to the colonies in North America.

OLD SUGAR HOUSE, NEAR GALLOWGATE.

But not all the rum that flowed into Britain was destined to stay there. British rum drinkers had a preference for the higher strength Jamaican rum. Barbados rum was mostly re-exported to other European territories. Demand was especially high in Ireland, which consumed more rum than England and Wales combined in the latter part of the 18th century.

YO HO HO

It's almost impossible to talk about rum without referencing pirates, but the significance of piracy in the story of rum is hugely overplayed. Real pirates were little more than rag-tag packs of ocean-going militia, comprising wandering criminals, social outcasts, and debtors, with bills that no honest man could pay. Some pirates operated as "privateers" – a form of legally sanctioned pirating, introduced by Elizabeth I to disrupt Spanish colonial efforts. Some of the famed wrongdoings of pirates and privateers are as legendary as they sound (see Captain Morgan on pages 192–93), but many of our perceived pirate stereotypes are either dramatic embellishments of the truth or just pure fiction.

The golden age of pirating came about at the end of the 17th century, which coincided with the first sugar plantations establishing themselves in the Caribbean. Rum was in a nascent state during this time; it was in production and available locally, but not yet the widely traded international commodity that it would soon become. The merchant ships of the late 17th century

LEFT Glasgow's second sugar refinery, called the Old Sugar House, was erected in 1669 by a group of Glasgow merchants to refine sugar imported from the Caribbean.

were more often packed with wine, French brandy and Dutch genever. And it's those drinks – not rum – that typically "shivered a pirate's timbers".

In fact, the association between pirates and rum was all but nonexistent until 1883, when Robert Louis Stevenson penned *Treasure Island*. Originally serialized in a children's magazine, the novel was written around 50 years after the last pirate had walked the plank. Stevenson probably had less reference material concerning rum and pirates to go on than we do today, and while the geographical connection between piracy and rum is easy to establish, it's highly unlikely that pirates were as committed to rum drinking as Stevenson would have us believe.

The word "rum" appears 57 times in *Treasure Island* ("brandy" appears just 14 times), and most famously on the opening page:

"Fifteen men on the dead man's chest - Yo-ho-ho, and a bottle of rum!"

This sea shanty, like most of the rest of his book, was a product of Stevenson's imagination, and these words were never consciously spoken by a pirate, or anyone else, until *Treasure Island* appeared on book shelves. It's alleged that Stevenson found the name "Dead Man's Chest" among a list of Virgin Island names in a book by fellow novelist Charles Kingsley, possibly in reference to the Dead Chest Island off Peter Island in the British Virgin Islands. It's likely that Stevenson's "bottle of rum" is the single greatest contributor to the rum-swigging pirate cliché, but rum wasn't the only piece of pirate mythology perpetuated by Stevenson. Treasure maps, gravel-throated west-country accents, and walking around with a parrot on one's shoulder are all creations of Stevenson's.

The image of the rum-guzzling pirate

ROBERT LOUIS STEVENSON'S
TREASURE ISLAND

:: ARTHUR BOURCHIER ::
As "LONG JOHN SILVER."

ABOVE A (barely) walking cliché of what a pirate probably wasn't. Except for the fact that in this instance, he is uncharacteristically without a bottle of rum.

has proved a difficult one to shake. Stevenson's book, along with fictional characters that it has influenced, such as Captain Hook from J.M. Barrie's *Peter Pan* and more recently Jack Sparrow from the *Pirates of the Caribbean* franchise, offer a glamorous portrayal of criminality on the high seas, where morals are loose and the rum flows freely. My favourite line from *Treasure Island* that concerns rum is delivered by Long John Silver himself. While recovering from a sword fight Silver refuses medical attention, insisting that rum will suffice, "I lived on rum, I tell you. It's been meat and drink, and man and wife, to me".

A RUM RATION

In the spring of 1655, English Vice-Admiral William Penn set sail from Barbados with a fleet of 37 war ships and several thousand soldiers. His intention was to take the island of Hispaniola from the Spanish, but the attack was ill-prepared and mismanaged. Penn was reluctant to return to Barbados with his tail between his legs, however, so he opted instead to sail further west, and attempt to seize the less desirable Spanish colony of Jamaica. This time he was successful, resulting in the establishment of what would, by the early 1700s, surpass Barbados as Britain's most valuable Caribbean territory. The capture of Jamaica on May 17 1655 also marked the start of a Royal Navy tradition that would remain in place for over one-third of a millennium: the rum ration.

Or so the story goes. In fact, there is no documented evidence to confirm that rum was rationed to troops in Jamaica. What we do know is that Jamaica was a tobacco island under Spanish rule, and grew only a token gesture of sugarcane to satisfy the local market. We also know that there are no accounts of rum production or rum consumption on the island prior to the arrival of the British in 1655. So it seems strange that the capture of Jamaica, of all places, served as the catalyst for the Navy rum ration, and especially so when one considers that the fleet had just sailed from Barbados – an island that was known to be producing cane spirits at that time! Even if rum was being made in Jamaica in 1655, it would only have been for local consumption, and in 1654 the population of Jamaica was just 2,500. Where then, would stocks of rum sufficient to fill the bellies of seven thousand British sailors be conjured up from?

There are solid historical references to rum rationing on ships at Port Royal, Jamaica, in the 1680s, and it's fair to assume that the practice was going on in Jamaica for some years prior to that. Given the island's dominance in both sugar and rum production in the 18th century, it would have been convenient for some historians to establish a link between the Royal Navy arriving there and rum appearing on-board their ships. But I for one think that it's likely that rum was not new to sailors in 1655 and that it was issued to them before the capture of Jamaica as well as afterwards.

One thing's for sure though: life on a 17th-century Royal Navy ship was a living hell. Squalid living conditions, biscuit rations, strict punishment and the constant fear of death by disease or hostile encounter. Alcohol was a necessary antidote on these voyages, and the traditional maritime appetite for alcohol was never more voracious than during this period when men were spending longer at sea than ever before. Sailors were dispensed beer rations at an agreeable rate of one gallon per day, but the beer was prone to turning sour after a couple of weeks at sea and that left only slimy water as a source of refreshment. Some time in the middle of the 17th century, sailors became acquainted with rum. In those days, Royal Navy ships operated autonomously and there was no standard regulations or code of instructions (seamen and even officers wouldn't have standardized uniform for another 100 years). So the practice likely began on a micro-level then spread steadily throughout the rest of the fleet as rum became more available. Rum (and other spirits) was the natural choice of

refreshment for sailors, because on long voyages it didn't go sour in the barrel – indeed, it improved!

Then there was the fact that it was strong stuff, which the sailing men no doubt approved of. We can only guess at the real strength of the spirit back then, though. Distillation techniques were mostly rather crude in the 17th century, and it wasn't until 1816 that Sikes's hydrometer was invented and the ability to measure strength (proof) accurately became a reality. The term "proof" (in its capacity as a gauge of alcoholic strength) originated in the Royal Navy, and more specifically with regard to rum. It was the task of the ship's purser (the supplies handler) to assess the quality of all incoming food and drink stocks from the port, as well as to manage their rationing among the men. Where rum was concerned, this meant testing the alcohol content to ensure that the liquid wasn't diluted by some unscrupulous trader wishing to squeeze some extra cash out of his client. The test was conducted using gunpowder, wherein the rum was mixed with a small quantity

of the powder and heated with an open flame. The burning of the gunpowder was observed by the purser, who gauged the ferocity of the flame to calculate the strength of the rum. There were no percentages or degrees on his scale, however – rum was either deemed strong enough or not. The test became known as the "proof" test. Rum that burned like dry gunpowder was "proven" to be of adequate strength, and that strength happened to be 57% alcohol by volume. Rum burning hotter or brighter than gunpowder was clearly stronger, and those rums were labelled "over-proof".

The Royal Navy demanded that all rums stored on Navy ships were over-proof. Perhaps this was because a barrel of "under-proof" rum spilt its contents all over an adjacent cask of gunpowder causing the gunpowder to burn poorly and rendering a ship defenceless. Or perhaps it was just the mariners hankering for the burn of strong spirit. The Navy's policy changed in 1866 when all Navy rum was prescribed at 4.5 under-proof, which is where it stayed for the duration of the ration.

From the mid-1600s until the 1730s, rum was rationed to sailors without rules or guidelines. In fact, there are very few accounts of rum rationing at all until the 18th century, and those that do exist are rather vague. In February 1727, Captain Gascoigne of the *HMS Greyhound*, which was stationed at Port Royal, wrote to the Navy Board suggesting that a "double allowance of rum" might encourage the men under his command to work harder.

In 1731, the first documented regulations "Relating to His Majesty's Service at Sea" were published, which reveal both what a daily rum ration constituted and that the ritual had spread beyond the Caribbean, into wider Royal Navy operations. The regulations stated that a standard issue gallon of beer was equivalent to "a pint of wine or half a pint of brandy, rum or arrack". Whether rum, brandy or arrack (which would have served as a substitute for rum or brandy in the East Indies), a half pint of strong spirit a day is equivalent to ten double shots (50 ml or 2 oz) – every day.

With that much alcohol flowing through a sailor's veins, it's amazing that sailors felt the need to smuggle extra stocks of rum on-board during shore leave. One trick commonly employed by shrewd seamen in the Caribbean involved emptying coconuts of their milk and refilling them with rum before boarding the ship. Extra drams were also occasionally issued by officers as rewards for exemplary service or acts of heroism. Before going into battle, captains sometimes ordered a "tot" (a ration) for the crew to make them more "brave and willing."

RUM, GROGGERY AND THE LASH

For many sailors, rum would become their only form of liquid intake, and was the cause of no shortage of accidents, disputes and deaths. But alcoholism was really only a single strand in a sorry tapestry of malnutrition and poor hygiene on-board Navy ships. During the 18th century diseases killed more British sailors than combat did, and the biggest killer of all was scurvy – a deficiency in vitamin C. One of the most horrendous examples of this was Vice-Admiral Hosier's siege of Portobello, which over a six-month period resulted in the death of 4,000 men from 'fever' compared to only a handful who died in battle.

This plight of the seaman was recognized by one man. Admiral Edward Vernon was adored by his men for his obvious concern for their wellbeing, and for his exceptional leadership skills in battle. Vernon petitioned for the rum ration to be reduced, but more crucially, that it should be mixed with water, limes and sugar. His pleas were heard, and in 1740 the rum issue became gospel. The concoction was served twice daily, once between 10am and 12pm, and another between 4pm and 6pm. This new drink needed a name, and with the sailors' known ability for inventive language, it

RIGHT Edward Vernon: Royal Navy Admiral, mixologist and grogram coat advocate.

RIGHT Not content with inventing "grog", Admiral Vernon achieved what Hosier couldn't, capturing Portobello in 1739.

was called "grog" – named for the grogram waterproof boat cloak that was the trademark apparel of Admiral Vernon.

With fresh lime juice featuring in the diet of every sailor in the Navy from 1740 onwards, there's no telling how many lives that would have otherwise been lost to scurvy were saved by Admiral Edward Vernon's cocktail. The mixture of rum to water (and other ingredients) was set at 4:1 in favour of water, but this was prone to change depending on who was in charge. As such, the mixture seamen used for grog was named by compass points. Due North was pure rum, and due West was water alone. WNW would therefore be one-third rum and two-thirds water, and NW half and half. If a seaman had two "nor-westers," he'd had two glasses of half rum and half water.

THE BLACK TOT

In the 19th century, there was a slow change of attitude towards intoxication among active servicemen. In 1824 the tot of rum was halved in size to one-quarter of a pint (one gill) and the sailors were compensated by an increase in pay and additional rationing of meat, cocoa and tea. As early as 1850 the Admiralty's "Grog Committee" met to discuss the problems associated with over-consumption of alcohol among seamen, and shortly after they released a report which confirmed the relationship between drunkenness and discipline, recommending that the ration be abolished. Rather than abolish it the Royal Navy Commission reduced it again, this time half a gill (one-eighth of a pint).

Following these reductions in quantity it seems that the Royal Navy took a greater interest in the quality of the rum. Since the inception of the tot, the Navy were prone to shop around, initially buying most of their stock from Jamaica and Barbados. But by the 19th century, their preference tended to lie with Guyana. From 1783 onwards all purchases were made through the sugar broker, ED & F Man & Co., who continued to supply the Navy right up until 1970 when the ration was abolished. In 1908 the Royal Navy purchased 420,000 gallons of "Demerara rum". All rum shipments were sent to the Royal Victoria Yard where they were blended in linked vats which were never entirely emptied. This brought a degree of consistency to the liquid, in much the same way as a solera system works (see page 69). James Park's *Nelson's Blood* (1983) details an account from one P. Curtis, who was a chief petty officer stationed at *HMS Terror* in Singapore shortly after World War II. He recounts an evening where no less than six chief pursers got together with various samples of blending stock and over the course of two hours of appreciating "the glow which spreads from the stomach and engenders that wonderful feeling of peace and bonhomie", they established a blend of rums that was agreed to be perfect by all present. The blend comprised: "fifty-five percent Demerara, thirty percent Trinidad, with the remainder from Natal and Mauritius."

But while Curtis and company were fine-tuning the taste and aroma of a Navy tradition three-hundred years in the making, other men, in offices, were again calling for the rum ration to be done away with. It had been over 100 years since the tot had been dropped to

half a gill, during which time the Navy had fought two world wars and built aircraft carriers and nuclear submarines. Yet still, all over the world, rum was dispensed twice daily to service men and women.

On January 28 1970, the "Great Rum Debate" took place in the House of Commons. Despite impassioned speeches from the likes of MP James Wellbeloved, who argued that, "there is some evidence from people who serve at sea in Her Majesty's ships and in the Merchant Navy that a tot of rum can have a stabilising effect upon the stomach, and this is indeed a matter of considerable importance", it was decided that the rum ration had no place in the modern Navy. July 31 1970 would forever more be known as "Black Tot Day", when the last pipe of "Up Spirits" was chimed and the final ration issued at 11am – 24 times, in 24 time zones, across the globe.

By contrast with other members of the Commonwealth, the Royal Australian Navy had already discontinued the rum ration nearly 50 years earlier, in 1921. Two other Commonwealth navies retained the rum ration after the Royal Navy abandoned it, however. But less than two years after Black Tot Day, March 31 1972 became the final day of the rum ration in the Royal Canadian Navy. The New Zealand Navy displayed an impressive level of commitment to the rum ration, holding out until February 27 1990.

By means of compensation, British seamen were allowed an extra can of beer as part of their ration. The remaining rum stocks (which were

LEFT British Royal Navy sailors grab the largest vessels they can get their hands on for their twice-daily issue of grog from the ship's rum tub.

mostly stored in casks) were put up for auction. They were bought by Chief Petty Officer Brian Cornford, who had served in Royal Navy submarines during World War II. Cornford had the ships drop their remaining supplies off at Gibraltar, where with the help of John Kania, a cellar master under his employment, they undertook the laborious task of decanting the barrels into 1-gallon (1.2-US gallon) earthenware flagons, which were wrapped in wicker, sealed with wax and date-stamped. The flagons were then sold on again, with many of them ending up in Gibraltar bars during the 1970s and 1980s. They are now much harder to get hold of, although I do have one in my collection which is wax stamped with the year 1956. I plan on cracking it open on July 31 2020 to mark the 50-year anniversary of Black Tot Day.

There are countless reports of rum still making an appearance during particularly cold military operations during the 1980s and 1990s. By this point it took the form of a bottle of Lamb's or Pusser's however, rather than the original wicker-covered 1-gallon demijohns. Trawling through the military internet forums these days, there is plenty of anecdotal evidence to support the notion that rum still has a place in the modern Navy. And while it may not be dispensed through the official channels it's clear that there's a lasting legacy of strong booze that's difficult to erase completely.

NEW ENGLAND RUM

Bourbon whiskey has been the spirit of the United States for the past 150 years, but long before the first farmers mashed the first corn, it was rum that filled the tavern cups.

As with the tropics, alcohol played an important role in the physical and mental conditioning of colonists, for whom it provided medicine and nourishment for both body and mind. Colonizing required its own set of skills, and re-establishing the psychological muscle memory of learned social rituals was key to the general mood of colonial society. Alcohol played its own part in this, and when coupled with the fact that colonists possessed a "deep seated distrust of water" (as Wayne Curtis puts it in his book *And a Bottle of Rum*), making one's own hooch was damn near essential.

So the colonists began brewing – beer mostly, from cereals, like rye and dark barley malts, but also from corn, apples, pumpkin and other fruits and fermentable sources. But these crops were needed for the equally important act of eating. So wines were imported too, from Portugal, Madeira and France, but this was not cheap. Not to mention that a dependence on Europe for your evening's night cap was, psychologically, a step backward rather than forward. What colonists really yearned for was the freedom and independence to work a hard day in the fields, and then drink hard, home-grown, liquor at night… (and sometimes in the day, too).

The first rum distillery was built on Staten Island, New York in 1650 (and a second in Boston in 1657), just a decade after the first Caribbean operations manifested themselves, and barely a generation after the Pilgrim Fathers established the colony of Massachusetts. Molasses arrived by boat from the Caribbean, where, at the time, there was an overwhelming surplus of the stuff, and once again it was the Dutch who provided the know-how to convert it into a strong spirit. And since rum was unlikely to have been traded by boat in any meaningful quantity until the late 1650s, it's fair to surmise that distilleries in Massachusetts and New York were inspired to make rum independently of their Caribbean cousins.

For colonies on Barbados and Martinique, early distilling was a simple means of leveraging value out of industrial waste, but in New York and Boston, no sugar mills existed, so the purchase of bulk shipments of molasses and the establishment of distilleries to process it testifies to the resourcefulness of the colonists where matters of high-strength alcohol were concerned.

In the space of a decade or so, rum was everywhere. As the population of the colonies increased, so too did the demand for rum, although this was at a far greater rate than the distilleries could keep up with. Rum was available in every tavern and tippling house, and it was drunk widely at home where it was also used in cooking – sometimes even finding its way into a recipe for "fryed bacon" – or when served once to Rev. Elijah Kellogg, "with salt fish and crackers". Rum was used as a currency – it was traded with native Americans for furs (and used as leverage once a dependency had been established), or as part payment of wages. Rum was made in and consumed in colonial towns, in scraggly half-built villages, halfway up mountains and in the remote northern ports around Newfoundland. Rum was produced domestically, but also flowed in from Barbados (which was considered to be the best rum-producing country of that time) along with regular shipments from Grenada and Antigua. Given that these spirits were no doubt shipped in barrels, the preference for imported spirit may have been down to the simple softening of the spirit by the oak cask.

Rum was the most widely consumed drink of its time. It was drunk on an abusive scale, which was likeable to London's disastrous "gin craze" of the early 1700s. By the middle of the 18th century, the average American adult was drinking a bottle-and-a-half of rum every week.

The most common way to do this was the easiest – straight-up and sometimes followed by a glass of water. Sometimes the water and rum were mixed before knocking it back, and when sweetened and spiced they formed a drink known as *mimbo*. More commonly it was mixed with molasses, where the drink was instead called *bombo*.

But cocktail etiquette was loose in those days, little was off-limits, and rum was mixed with anything that was found lying around: it was mixed with shrub vinegars in a "Switchel", mixed with hard cider in a "Samson" and combined with beaten eggs in a "Bellowstop". But the best drink of the era was unquestionably the "Flip", which required some equipment, however. It consisted of a large earthenware bowl, to which rum, sugar (or molasses), ale and spices were added. The mixture would be stirred before – in a most dramatic turn of events – a hot "loggerhead" was stabbed into its murky depths. A loggerhead is a kind of fire poker with a ball on the end, which tended to be the first weapon men went for during drunken brawls (hence the phrase "at loggerheads"). But this wasn't all about theatre; the use of the hot loggerhead affected the drink in a number of ways: first – and most obviously – it heats it, though not to the point of it being a "hot" drink, but rather a "warm" one. The intense heat also causes the bubbles in the beer to expand, which foams up the drink, adding a bit of drama to

proceedings. Finally, the heat of the loggerhead also cooks the drink, caramelizing the sugars and creating Maillard reactions, that contribute toasty, cooked, qualities. The caramelization also produces bitter flavours, that in turn balance the sweetness of the beer and sugar.

The Flip existed in a time before the widespread hopping of beer, and this searing process introduced some of the bitterness that hop flowers would normally provide. Combine all of the above elements together: sweetness, aromatic spice, homely cereal notes, fruitiness, gentle warmth, foamy texture and a more-ish bitterness, and you're left with one of the great drinks of all time – produced using only blacksmith's tools and the foraged scraps of an adolescent colonial society.

THE REVOLUTIONARY SPIRIT

"I know not why we should blush to confess that Molasses was an essential Ingredient in American Independence. Many great Events have proceeded from much smaller causes."

John Adams, second President of the United States

The North American molasses trade was a useful little earner for the British Caribbean planters, who charged 10p (£20 or $27 today) a gallon for the stuff. The British Empire was highly attentive to the needs of these powerful business leaders, and therefore keen to maintain a healthy trade between colonies. But the North Americans were a savvy bunch, and in the pursuit of favourable prices, they soon began trading with the entire Caribbean region and especially the French. Saint-Domingue, Martinique and Guadeloupe sold molasses at around half the price of the British product – a bargain only made possible by a surplus of product and favourable re-export tariffs set by the French government to curb the enormous quantities of sugar and molasses that was landing in French mainland ports. By 1730, the colony of Massachusetts was importing over 90 per cent of its molasses requirements from the French West Indies.

The British planters were not happy about this, and in response, the British parliament introduced the Molasses Act in 1733. The Act imposed a tax on molasses imported from foreign colonies, such as the French or Dutch West Indies, at a rate of 6p (£12 or $20 today) per gallon. This brought the price of a gallon to around 10p (£20 or $27 today) regardless of where you bought it from. This did not sit well with New England and the other colonies. Rum was the currency of the North America trading enterprise, but more than that it was a manufactured item that was of their own making, not imported, not a hand out, but representative of the blood and sweat of the overall colonial endeavour. History teaches us that there's a fine balance to be had where matters of tax on alcohol (or products related to the production of alcohol) are concerned. If actually collected, the molasses tax would have slowed economic growth in New England and destroyed much of the rum industry in the process. In this instance the tax was poorly policed and expertly evaded. This was one of the first examples of mass civil disobedience among the colonists, and cited by some historians as the first murmuring of revolutionary uprising.

Three decades passed and an average of only £2,000 (£400,000 or $660,000 today) of tax revenue was collected each year. By the 1760s, the British were strapped for cash following the Seven Years' War (1754–63), which had doubled the national debt. In response, parliament raised taxes on many imported goods, but also passed a modified version of the Molasses Act. The ensuing Sugar Act of 1764 halved the rate of taxation on molasses, but on this occasion Britain was going to make damn sure it was paid. Policing was overseen by the British Army and a fleet of 27 mobile Royal Navy ships who were permitted to pursue smugglers on the high seas. The Act also throttled the trade in timber and other colonial goods with French colonies.

Just like the earlier Molasses Act, this new legislation was an enormous threat to the American rum industry, which by this point was making 80% of its 6 million gallons (22 million litres) of annual consumption from imported molasses. The colonists, who viewed the new Act as a great injustice, took to the streets with placards and pamphlets. In what could almost be classed as a "democratic" turn of events, the tax was

RIGHT The so-called Boston Tea Party is often seen as the catalyst for the American Revolution, but the revolutionary seed was planted by sugar, molasses and rum.

reduced (in 1766) to just 1p (£2 or £3.50 today) a gallon. But this rollback of taxation policy represented a major paradigm shift in the relationship between colonist and crown. A growing sense of fortitude seasoned the punch bowls of New England taverns, and rum nurtured the first stirrings of dissent. Aware that they had buckled in the face of popular demand, Parliament launched a counter-offensive and imposed direct taxes on the colonies for the first time. The Stamp Act of 1765 required colonists to pay tax on every piece of printed paper they used. The Tea Act of May 1773 granted the British East India Company a monopoly on tea sales in the American colonies. The cry went out across the colonies "no taxation without representation!"

The iconic Boston Tea Party took place six months later, in December 1773 during which the Sons of Liberty destroyed a huge shipment of East India Company tea. In February 1775, Parliament declared Massachusetts to be in a state of rebellion, and in April of that year conflicts broke out, commencing with battles at Lexington and Concord. The American Revolutionary War had begun.

FINDING SUCCESS IN THE 19TH CENTURY

Up until the middle of the 19th century, the sugar business remained the dominant economic activity across all but the smallest of the Caribbean islands. But the abolition of the Atlantic slave trade by the European colonial powers between 1807 and 1818, followed by the Slavery Abolition Act of 1833, which outlawed slavery in the British Empire, demanded a rapid transition for planters from slave labour to a free labour system.

This necessitated profound changes in the running of plantations and distilleries, from recruitment to welfare and workforce management. The upshot was that making sugar was going to cost more money from now on. In addition to workforce challenges, the productivity of Caribbean sugar estates was beginning to suffer thanks to soil exhaustion, which had rendered entire sections of Barbados unsuitable for growing sugarcane by the 1820s. This had a positive impact on Demerara sugar, however, which if left unchecked threatened to flood the market and destabilize commodity prices.

This came at a time when Europe, and especially France, was busy developing an alternate sugar source: sugar beets. By 1837, there were 542 sugar beet factories in France producing 35,000 tons (38,600 US tons) of raw sugar annually. By 1890 over half the world's sugar came from sugar beet. This increased the global availability of sugar and lowered its value at a time when plantations cost more than ever to run.

The old system was broken, the financial margins simply didn't add up, and the business plan needed a drastic re-write. Hundreds of small mills (and distilleries) across the British Caribbean closed during this period, or were consolidated into larger industrial operations. Others ceased refining activities but doggedly persevered with rum production. This set the stage for the next turn in rum's long journey as the islands attempted to commercialize their distilleries in a world that wouldn't stand still.

Fortunately, the industrial age was there to help, revolutionizing distillery technology and shaping rum flavour in the process. Rum-making methods hadn't evolved much in three centuries, and the pot still followed the same basic distillation principles that had been established in the ninth century. Rum was still produced in batches, which was time-consuming and costly, and highly prescriptive as far as the final flavour of the spirit was concerned. A continuous still was needed; a device that could process fermented beer or wine and turn it into high-strength alcohol without all the faffing about.

The first attempt at this came from an illiterate Frenchman by the name of Edouard Adam, who patented a prototype continuous still in 1804. Adam's column was a horizontal arrangement that linked together a series of what Adam called "large eggs", with pipes that would route alcohol vapour from one egg to the next. The design is highly reminiscent of the pot still and retort set ups that are still used in some rum distilleries today.

The column-shaped Pistorius still arrived in 1817. The pioneering design was adapted the following year by Dutch sugar trader Armand Savalle, which in turn became a popular design among rum distillers, especially in the French Caribbean. Later versions were developed by the French engineer Jean-Baptiste Cellier-Blumenthal, and Robert Stein, the owner of the Kilbagie distillery in Fife, Scotland.

Then, in 1830, came the revolutionary design patented by the Irishman Aeneas Coffey. The Coffey still was the first of its kind to sustain a truly continuous process of distillation. It was a work of genius for its time, as evidenced by the fact that the same basic design is used in many distilleries today.

The French and Spanish rum-makers were the earliest adopters of the continuous still, while the British stuck to their pots. This tactic proved successful (for the time being) as the trademark high-ester Jamaican style became a spirit category in its own right. Export volumes reached all-time highs and the cash piled up, so much so that it garnered the attention of great chemists and engineers, who applied scientific principles to rum-making through research into yeast, fermentation and dunder (see pages 58–60). They sought to understand the nuances of rum production, with the aim of broadening rum styles as tastes shifted to lighter styles. By the end of the century, Jamaican distillers were producing high- and low-ester marques, and rum export values outpaced that of sugar.

The French island of Martinique

LEFT Despite the gradual decline of the sugar industry on Barbados, there were still dozens of sugar estates at the end of the 19th century, like Spring Hall in St. Lucy.

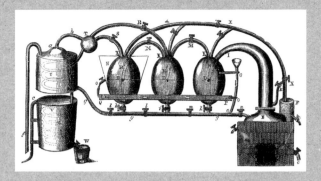

RIGHT Edouard Adam's still formed the basis of the first truly continuous stills, but it also possessed similar features to many of the pot still and retorts that are used today to make "heavier" rums.

experienced a similar trajectory of growth, with exports increasing by a factor of 20 between 1850 and 1890. This unprecedented surge in uptake was largely due to the devastation of European vineyards by the *phylloxera* mite. When wine and brandy stocks dwindled, the French looked to the colonies for a source of hard liquor, and Martinique was only too happy to oblige.

The arrival of the continuous still divided the rum- producing world into two camps: those with pots and those without. Lighter styles were considered purer and therefore higher in quality, while pot-still rums developed a reputation for being smelly and rough. A style somewhere in the middle of the two was deemed to be something that most people would get along with nicely. But these heavy and light rums were limited by the equipment that was used to make them. The solution presented itself eventually and gave rise to a new faction within the rum canon: blenders.

Blending was a British invention, and one that would later become synonymous with Scotch whisky. With America's attentions shifted to whiskey production, and the Royal Navy fully invested in dramming, rum was becoming a drink with increasingly British associations.

Blenders established themselves on both sides of the Atlantic, applying a degree of credibility to the liquor where there was once none. Blending stretched volumes of good-quality stuff and covered up the not so good ones. But more than anything, it gave a guarantee of quality and authenticity.

A RUM SUPERPOWER

The arrival of the column still in Cuba set the stage for a new, lighter, cleaner style of rum that would become the hallmark of the best-selling rum brands in the world today. Cuban rum captured the imagination of the US, helped to establish rum's relevance within cocktail culture and fostered the development of some of the world's best bartenders (not to mention bars) in the early 20th century.

In an age of Martinis and Champagne, light rum was a necessary deviation for a category heavily rooted in, well, heaviness. Light rum didn't need to be tamed with aggressive flavours, or blended down. This rum was for mixing, sipping and swigging back from a highball as you mambo across the dance floor.

The continuous still came at just the right time for the Spanish islands, where distilleries began popping up in the late 18th century. Lucrative trading with the newly independent US meant that islands like Cuba quickly became the most industrially advanced in the region. In the 19th century, sugar- and rum-making were enterprises tied directly to Cuba's social and economical successes or failures. Geographically dislocated from its Spanish motherland, Cuba was also a world away in terms of its drinking habits. The rum made in Cuba became a product that could legitimately be called "Cuban" and that helped to establish the concept of identity and individuality among the Cuban people. Rum still resonates strongly on this island, because of the countless families of Spanish origin that helped to establish the Cuban identity by making and selling rum made from Cuban molasses.

By the 1860s, there were a remarkable 1,365 distilleries on Cuba, and the island exported 20.5 million litres (5.4 million US gallons) of rum each year – providing much-needed succour to soldiers during the American Civil War – and placing Cuba only behind Martinique in the rum rankings. So far as sugar was concerned, Cuba became the top producer in the world, outpacing Jamaica and all the other British colonies combined.

Cuba fought three wars against the Spanish between 1868 and 1898, culminating in a US-assisted victory and the agreement of Spain to relinquish all claim of sovereignty over the island. The Cuba libre trade-off heralded a new era of aggressive American influence that shaped the geopolitical landscape of the north Caribbean for decades to come. American sponsorship also helped to shape the sugar industry on Cuba, consolidating mills and distilleries into larger industrial operations that churned out rum at record-breaking levels. Finally, it transformed Havana into a party town that was seen by some as chic and sophisticated, and by others as an intoxicant of the soul, with its casinos, cocktail coupes, and the greatest bartenders of the age: the *cantineros*.

Cocktail culture was already well-

BELOW Carnival time in Havana, Cuba: a great opportunity to drink Cuban rum and drive fast cars in a circle.

BELOW RIGHT Bacardi adverts in Cuba in the 1940s stated "El Que a Cuba Ha Hecho Famosa" (The one that has made Cuba famous).

CARNIVAL TIME, HAVANA, CUBA.

established in many American cities by this point, but had failed to penetrate the colonial Caribbean because there was little call for it. Havana was just 160 km (100 miles) from Key West in Florida, and only a few hours by plane (once commercial air travel was established) from New York or Washington. At a time when the Temperance movement was gathering pace in the US, Cuba became the "local bar" of America. When Prohibition took effect in the US in 1920, America brought cocktail culture to the Cuban party and Cuba supplied all the rum. A joint advertising campaign between Bacardí and Pan Am airlines gave birth to such slogans as, "Leave the Dry Lands Behind," and "Fly to Cuba and Bathe in Bacardí rum." The tourism to the island doubled in a period of ten years, growing from 45,000 annual visitors in 1916 to 90,000 in 1926.

At that time, most of the (good) hotels in Havana were under the ownership of US companies, and the city became an intimate hotbed of various exotic vices complete with race track, sporting arenas and theme parks (it could be argued that Havana was a theme park) all serviced by the indebted Cuban populace. One of the better outcomes of this arrangement

was some of the greatest rum cocktails in the world today: Mojito (see pages 103–105), Daiquiri (see pages 112–113), El Presidente (see pages 124–125) and Mulata, to name but a few.

These drinks, while based on formulae of older whiskey- or gin-based cocktails, were conceived and executed by the *cantineros*, who tended bar for some of the greatest names of the era. The journalist Hector Zumbado described these celebrity service industry professionals as "Diplomatic, polyglot, like skilled ambassadors. Discreet and reserved."

The bars of this era are just as legendary as the men who tended them: the famed Havana establishment Sloppy Joe's – where the *cantineros* were known to make 100 daiquiris in a single (large) shaker – diverted its attentions from food to drink during Prohibition. La Floridita became "La Cuna del Daiquiri" ("The Cradle of the Daiquiri") under the legendary Constantino Ribalaigua Vert, who captained the bar team from 1918.

The Asociacion de Cantineros de Cuba served as a bartenders' trade union that operated apprentice schemes, ran extensive training programs and even trained bartenders in English, which was essential if they were to service the parched throngs of incoming American and British vacationers.

Prohibition established the market for Cuban rum in America, and once it was repealed, the American appetite for a "cleaner" style of rum endured – evident in the rise of even more neutral vodka. The Cuban approach spread through other rum-producing regions, even influencing distilleries which had in the past been stalwarts of the pot-still approach, such as Trinidad. Cuban rum endured too, but more through its most famous progeny, Bacardí, and its legacy as the modern rum standard, than as an island of rum distillers.

WAR AND SURVIVAL

As the Cuban spirit soared, the first decade of the 20th century was a complete disaster for Martinique, which up until that point had remained the world's biggest rum producer. The eruption of Mount Pelée, on May 8 1902 wiped out dozens of distilleries that surrounded Sainte-Pierre – touted the rum capital of the world – and export volumes from the island dropped from 18 million litres (4.8 million US gallons) in 1901 down to around half that in 1903. The decade that followed became a period of consolidation, as the surviving distilleries took the opportunity to snap up smaller plantations and increase their production capacities. These larger molasses distilleries became known as producers of *rhum industriel* while the older, smaller operations that tended to farm and juice their own cane, produced *rhum agricole*.

Meanwhile, the British Caribbean sugar industry was in its death throes, as competition from rival sugar beet and Central and South American producers saw commodity prices plummet. The entire industry had been flipped on its head: sugar was no longer the high-value spice that it had once been, but the spirit formerly known as "Kill Devil" was becoming a premium product! Trinidad switched to oil, Grenada to spices and Barbados to tourism; all maintained distilling operations, but for the time being, their respective rum markets contracted to local trade only.

Guyana began to mine bauxite (aluminium ore), which competed with sugar for economic dominance. However, the sugar industry survived thanks to biannual harvests, a quality product and the importation of cheap labour: over 250,000 Indians between

RIGHT The catastrophic eruption of Martinique's Mount Pelée in 1902 destroyed the town of Saint-Pierre, engulfing some of the biggest and best rum distilleries in the Caribbean at that time.

the latter 19th and early 20th centuries. Large wholesale contracts from British blenders also kept rum distilleries working in spite of continued consolidation.

In Jamaica, the Sugar Experiment Station opened in 1905. It had the aim of perfecting the agriculture of sugarcane on the island, as well as exploring the potential for further diversity in Jamaican rum. Quality improved, and the European market maintained a healthy demand for it. In spite of this, 80 Jamaican distilleries closed in the first half of the 20th century.

World War I supercharged rum production across the region, as the French government issued rations of *rhum agricole* to an army of 1 million soldiers. Approximately 136 million litres (36 million US gallons) of rum were exported from Martinique during the war, accounting for 75% of the island's export revenue. British rum was drunk in French trenches too. When water came up to your knees it was no doubt a welcome respite from the misery of trench warfare, leading to one British soldier to remark, "Rum of course is our chief great good. The Ark of the Covenant was never borne with greater care than is bestowed upon the large stone rum-jars in their passage through this wilderness."

Despite the growth of bourbon, rum production in the US continued into the 20th century, and nowhere more so than in the former British colonies of New England and Massachusetts. Prohibition put an end to that of course, but it was not the only disaster to befall the US rum business.

January 15 1919 was an unusually warm day in Boston, which might have been why the US Industrial Alcohol Distilling Company tank, which was filled with 16 million litres (2.3 million US gallons) of molasses, decided to buckle, spilling its contents into the streets and harbour. The flood killed 21 individuals and injured more than 150 others while damaging an estimated $1 million (£6 million or $10 million today) of property. The 1919 tragedy inundated the newpapers with conspiracies and conjecture about how the tank had failed so epically. It is even said that on a hot summer's day, there is still a lingering scent of molasses in the North End and around Commercial Street.

The rest of the Spanish-speaking Caribbean adopted Cuban techniques in an effort to exploit the growing market for Cuban rum. Rum distilleries multiplied in Puerto Rico during the early part of the century and the Dominican rum industry flourished thanks to an influx of Cuban workers in the 1880s. New distilleries popped up across Central America too, in Panama (1922) Nicaragua (1937), and Guatemala (1939) – all of them leveraging the American appetite for lighter rum.

FULL CIRCLE

By the end of the 16th century, sugarcane had crossed the Pacific and arrived back to the islands from which it originated, leaving a trail of war, taxation, trade and culture in its wake. The Americas continued to dominate the industry, right up until the end of the 19th century, but Asia would soon become the sweetest spot on earth. Of the top five sugarcane growers in the world today, four are Asian (though even combined, they do not match the colossal production levels of Brazil – the world's top producer).

Wherever sugarcane could grow, rum was never far behind. In South Africa, rum was known simply as "cane". In Dutch Indonesia, cane was used (along with palm) to make a similar spirit to rum called *arrack*.

Sugarcane arrived in Australia in 1788, on the ships of the First Fleet. Through the colony's first 25 years, until the first coins were minted in 1813, rum was New South Wales' *de facto* form of currency. When the first permanent regiment (the New South Wales Corps) arrived in 1790, they served as both colonial enforcer and financial regulator, overseeing the importation and distribution of rum among the colonists and getting rather rich off the back of it. This led to their nicknaming as the "Rum Corps".

In 1806, Governor William Bligh arrived in New South Wales, a man already written in legend for his part in the Mutiny on the Bounty – the notorious incident in which he and 18 loyalists were set adrift by acting Lieutenant Fletcher Christian and forced to survive on rum rations as they travelled 6,500 km (3,500 nautical miles) to reach safety. Bligh's leadership qualities once again proved to be fuel enough for a revolt, when the Rum Corps staged the Rum Rebellion, deposing Governor Bligh who had attempted to destroy illegal stills and curtail the quantity of overpriced rum that filtered through the Corps' cellars. The Rum Rebellion is the first and only instance of the overthrow of the Australian government.

Australia was so far away from the Caribbean and Europe that most of the imported rum came via India or Java. Casks of Bengal rum (which was reputed to be stronger than Jamaican rum) were in the hold of nearly every ship from India, and Indian merchants grew wealthy thanks to the Sydney trade, sending their ships "laden half with rice and half with bad spirits", according to the Australian historian Geoffrey Blainey.

The popularity of rum "down under" didn't falter, and the island's first legitimate sugar mills and rum distilleries were built in northern Queensland in the 1860s. The view was taken that white men lacked the stamina to work the plantations, so an estimated 62,000 labourers were brought to Queensland between 1863 and 1904. Virtually all of them came from the indigenous populations of New Guinea, Vanuatu, the Solomon Islands and the New Hebrides – Australia was one of the last places on earth to cultivate sugarcane, but its workforce was supplied by one of the first.

In 1869, the world's first and only mobile rum distillery was born: the *SS Walrus* was taken over by the Pioneer Floating Sugar Company and fitted out with a working sugar mill and distillery. It travelled up and down the Albert and Logan Rivers in Queensland, anchoring at wharves near the cane fields. The mill was capable of crushing 2 tons (2.2 US tons) of sugar a day and used the leftover molasses to make rum. As ingenious as a floating rum distillery sounds, it was a failure. Distilling operations ceased in 1871 and the ship was decommissioned two years later. The oldest surviving legal distillery in Australia is Beenleigh, Queensland, which was originally founded by Francis Gooding and John Davy in 1884 – a time when there were over a dozen rum distilleries in Queensland.

Distillation in the Philippines has a history dating back to the 16th century, but the nation's first rum distillery was born out of an old *aguardiente* (a strong spirit, translating as "fiery water", which

is often made from sugarcane) and "tuba"(a type of palm wine) distillery in Hagonoy. In 1856, the distillery was acquired by Valentin Teus y Yrisarry and, six years later, a rectifying plant was built in Isla de Tanduay.

By the 1930s, the rum produced here was branded as "Tanduay Rhum" and its packaging was changed from the 45-litre (10-gallon) *dama juana* container to the more practically sized 750-ml (25-oz) glass bottles. Tanduay is the third highest selling rum brand in the world today.

In the Indian Ocean, the Madine Distillery Company was established on the volcanic island of Mauritius in 1926 and has survived along with a further five distilleries (Charamel, Rhumerie de Mascareignes, Gray's, Oxenham and St. Aubin) taking the island's total to six – and that doesn't include the blenders! Sugarcane was introduced to Mauritius by the Dutch via Java, and the earliest record of rum distillation takes us back to 1850 and one Pierre Charles François Harel. The island produces both molasses and cane juice rums, and exports around 600,000 litres (160,000 US gallons) a year at present.

Nearby Réunion has an even longer history of rum, with the first stills arriving in 1704. The first modern distillery was set up by Frenchman Charles Panon-Desbassayns, and by 1842 there were 12 sugar mills and six distilleries on the island.

By 1928 that number had increased to 31 distilleries, 16 of which had sugar mills attached to them. The collapse of trade with occupied France during World War II forced the closure of two of the mills and all of the distilleries save for Isautier distillery which was founded by Charles Isautier in 1845. The Isautier distillery remains in operation today, run by the sixth generation of the family. Only two others have survived, and both of them are now subsidiaries of Group Quartier Français: Savanna distillery, which was originally established in 1870, and Rivière du Mât. The latter two produce the most famous rum brand on the island: Rhum Charrette.

TIKI TIME

Caribbean tourism started in 1778 when the Bath Hotel and Spring House were built on the island of Nevis. Further resorts appeared on the Bahamas, Barbados, Cuba and Jamaica in the late

19th century – destinations that were serviced by regular steam boat charters from the US. The rise of air travel and the availability of residential air conditioning, in the early 20th century, encouraged further tourism to the region, transporting those who could afford it to paradisiacal islands that offered an imaginative alternative to monochrome America.

Those who were less well-off were no less desirous for the same experience, and this was the catalyst of an American trend towards Hawaiian music, as well as the renaissance of 19th-century "tropical" literature, such as *Moby Dick* and *Treasure Island*. Cocktail bars, like the Coconut Grove in Los Angeles's Ambassador Hotel, capitalized on the fad, installing plastic palm trees and bringing island magic to the Hollywood set. But this was still the domain of the Martini and black-tie – a place for dancing and sipping, and largely indistinguishable from any other stylish nightclub of the era.

Then tiki came along.

With its roots in South Pacific mythology, tiki is best known for its flaming torches and wild-looking humanoid statues (or totems). For the rum lover, the cult of tiki grew to a similarly reverential status, mostly through the actions of a pair of American restaurant operators, who infused various elements of island culture into a no-frills, marketable product. For a mid-century American, tiki represented the thrill of being transported elsewhere – away from the office, the hardships of war, the anonymity of white spirits and moderation. Rum – with its associations with island life and the laid-back culture that comes with that (and of course sugar's ancient origins in Polynesia) – made it a perfect pairing for the grass-skirt revolution.

By the late 1950s, glass buoys, *exotica* music and drinks as big as your head were available in dozens of cities across the US and beyond. Two men in particular built thatched-roof empires off the back of tiki: Ernest Raymond Beaumont Gantt aka "Donn Beach" and Victor Bergeron aka "Trader Vic".

Gantt was born in Texas, but he left home young, touring the Caribbean with his grandfather for a few years,

LEFT Hawaii became an American territory in 1898, by which point it was a significant grower of sugarcane. It became a major tourist destination in the age of jet travel.

RIGHT Tiki had its roots firmly planted in Polynesia, but the rum all came from the Caribbean.

then, when Prohibition took effect, he became a bootlegger, smuggling contraband rum into the US from the Bahamas. In the 1930s, Gantt moved to Hollywood, and once Prohibition was repealed, he opened a bar in an old tailor's store called "Don's Beachcomber" (the name was later changed to "Don the Beachcomber's"). It was a modestly sized place, but charming to look at with its ramshackle array of artefacts that Gantt had salvaged along his travels: carved masks, flotsam, puffer fish and other marine ephemera.

The drinks lineup started out as a modest punch-style offering, but soon extended as Gantt (who by now was officially known as "Donn Beach") experimented with potent spices, tropical fruit juices and his own blend of rums. This was revolutionary mixology for the time, orchestrated by a man who had a deep understanding of how ingredients could be layered and paired – a philosophy that later became known as Don's "Rhum Rhapsodies".

As the catalogue of popular original cocktails expanded, Donn became increasingly secretive about the recipes, just as his rivals became ever more intent on obtaining them. To that end, his bartenders constructed the cocktails using coded or numbered bottles, the contents of which were unknown to them. Rum was personally selected by Donn, usually arriving from Jamaica or Guyana.

In 1937 a one-legged man named Victor Bergeron took an interest in Don the Beachcomber's bar. Bergeron was a San Francisco native who had opened a restaurant called Hinky Dinks in Oakland in 1934. The 30-capacity venue was inspired by Vic's trips to Cuba where he had met La Floridita's legendary cantinero Constante. As such, it was Cuban sandwiches and daiquiris on the menu at Hinky Dinks.

Vic was even more inspired by the multi-sensory spectacle that was Don the Beachcomber's, however, to the point where he offered to go into partnership with Donn. His proposal was rebuffed, though. Then, one day, in 1937, he closed Hinky Dinks, reopening and reinventing it as Trader Vic's.

Vic reinvented himself too, assuming the persona of "Trader Vic" and all the imaginative backstory that came with it. No longer was it a childhood bout of tuberculosis that had lost him a leg – instead it was the result of shark attack. Vic regaled his patrons with numerous tall tales of "The Trader's" adventures, most of them occurring in places that Vic wouldn't actually experience for some years to come. As flimsy as most ~ of his stories were, it didn't matter. Vic was the consummate businessman and like layers of teak veneer, Vic constructed a substantial brand, putting himself right at the centre of it.

Vic expanded his operations in the 1940s, to Seattle, then Beverly Hills, then on to the most iconic of all Trader Vic outposts: San Francisco. This four-storey operation was largely a food-led destination, curiously specializing in Cantonese cuisine. There were bars there too, of course, dispensing all manner of rum-spiked concoctions from the Dr. Funk (made with "Jamaica or Martinique" rum and pastis) to the Flamingo (made with "Puerto Rican rum, Angostura bitters, cucumber rind, and 7-Up") all served in brightly coloured vases, garnished with flowers and large, elaborate pieces of tropical plant matter.

By the early 1960s, there were 20 Trader Vic's across the US and around the same number of Don the Beachcomber's, too. Sadly for Donn, he didn't own most of them. Divorce lost him the rights to the business and further expansion was overseen by his ex-wife Sunny Sund. Donn went and fought in World War II, and upon his return, settled in Oahu, Hawaii, finding some success in taking tiki culture back

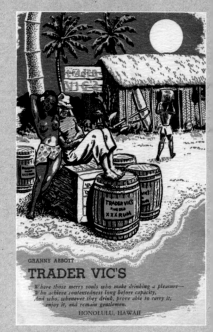

GRANNY ABBOTT

TRADER VIC'S

*Where those merry souls who make drinking a pleasure –
Who achieve contentedness long before capacity,
And who, whenever they drink, prove able to carry it,
enjoy it, and remain gentlemen.*

HONOLULU, HAWAII

ABOVE Trader Vic's and Don the Beachcomber's were successful because they didn't just sell food and drink – they offered a form of escape.

to where it all began.

By the 1970s tiki and cocktail culture in general were already in decline. When mixed drinks re-emerged in the 1980s, the legacy of tiki was present – in the drinks themselves, in their striking, almost ostentatious appearance and in their ludicrous names. If only the attention to ingredients displayed by Donn and Vic was there too. It was the dawn of the dark age of drinking.

THE NEW REVOLUTION

In the late 20th century, global rum sales remained largely stagnant but the sales split shifted considerably. Small distilleries across the Caribbean dropped like flies, through consolidation deals, or from being priced out of the market by favourable tariffs and tax breaks for larger operations. Rum became a bulk wholesale product. Great chunks of rum history were misplaced when these operations closed, taking with them centuries of traditional practices that are all but absent from the Caribbean today. With no clear route as to where rum had come from, the entire concept of rum became obscured. The cry went out, "what is rum?"

For many (like my parents) it was a colonial relic from a pre-industrial era; potent, pungent and consumed only by an older generation. For many others, it was Bacardí – a multinational brand that transcended the entire category. The message was incoherent and it set rum back an entire generation.

Then, finally, it seemed as though the fog was beginning to clear. In the first decade of the new millennium, rum was the fastest growing major spirit category in the world, with sales increasing by 40% over the 10-year period. Most of the growth was seen in Asia, which is now the biggest rum-drinking market in the world. Consumption doubled there between 2000 and 2010, thanks to emerging local brands like McDowell's No. 1 Celebration, which is not only India's most popular rum, but, as of 2015, the biggest- selling rum brand in the world – shifting 17.8 million 9-litre (2.4-US gallon) cases over the year.

But what about premium rum? Whisky, Cognac, vodka and gin – all had achieved some level of premiumization in the 1990s. Now, in the new millennium, it was rum's time to shine.

New releases from old distilleries trickled in, taking a lead from whisky and Cognac. These were fancily packaged products claiming good provenance and long maturation. Spiced rums were introduced and Barbados and Trinidad experienced a revival. Then new, aged releases followed from the French-speaking islands, the Spanish-speaking islands, Latin America and beyond. Realization set in: rum was being produced across dozens of countries, in numerous styles, and now at a broad range of prices.

In Europe, Spain and Germany are the largest rum markets and Spain is by far the biggest consumer of aged rum, with the market currently dominated by Brugal and Barcélo brands from the Dominican Republic. France and UK lean towards white rum, but aged rum, along with spiced offerings, is the fastest growing section of the category. Globally, the market for spiced and flavoured rums has doubled over the past 10 years, and it's these spirits that fill the glasses of the next generation of drinkers. Spiced rum now accounts for 8% of the total global rum category.

This diversity is cause for great celebration, but the absence of enforceable overarching legislation has also become one of rum's biggest challenges in the 21st century. In all the revolutionary excitement, no-one remembered to strategize the correct approach to marketing "new rum". Rather, rum brands have blindly snatched at cues from Scotch and vodka categories, recycling them into an abstract of rum.

The category has undoubtedly rediscovered itself – and yet, the question is still valid, "what is rum?" It's a spirit made from sugarcane products and sometimes aged in barrels. It is the most diverse spirit category in the world today. It's a consumer product that has shaped the geopolitical and cultural landscape of our world more than any other.

PART TWO
HOW RUM IS MADE

THE SCIENCE OF THE SUGARCANE

Sugarcane is a giant of the *Gramineae* (grass) family, certain varieties of which can grow up to 6 metres (20 ft) tall. The green leaves of the plant look like giant blades of grass, but the stem has a similar appearance to bamboo (also a member of the grass family) with a stem comprising interconnecting boney-looking joints, known as nodes. Each stem is typically 3–4 metres (10–13 ft) in height and about 5 cm (2 in) in diameter. Thanks to its size and leaf surface-area-to-mass ratio, sugarcane is a champion photosynthesizer. In the prime sugarcane-growing regions of the tropics, a single square metre (11 square feet) of sunshine can produce up to 17 kg (37 lbs) of sugarcane in a season.

And we're going to need it. It's estimated that the world will consume 174 million tons (191 US tons) of sugar in 2017 and around 80% of that sugar will be extracted from cane, the remainder coming from sugar beets. Both of these plants are unusual because they store energy in the form of sucrose instead of starch. Starch is the energy of choice for the rest of the plant kingdom because it isn't water soluble and doesn't draw water into the storage cells. In the case of sugarcane, this sucrose is dissolved into fluid in the stem of the plant. Good news for us, but bad news if you're short on water, because sugarcane needs a lot.

Shortly after the cane has flowered, it stockpiles sugar in preparation for growth in the following year, but if you cut it down at the right time, it's possible to literally raid the candy store. Thanks to centuries of continued cane cutting, the plant has retaliated by packing even more sugar into its stem, to the point where around one-fifth of its pressed juice is pure sugary goodness.

AGRICULTURE AND TERROIR

Being a grass has its advantages. One of which is that the plant does not require annually re-seeding. If cut correctly, the leftover stub will send up new stalks (called a *ratoon*) each season for up to 10 years. Successive harvests give decreasing yields however, so after 4–6 seasons it becomes necessary to replant the entire field. Mechanically harvested fields require more frequent replanting.

Cane *terroir* (a term that describes the soil, topography, and climate of environment in which the plant is grown) and cane variety is far less of a concern for rum producers that use molasses as their base material than it is for *rhum agricole* (see page 57) distillers or those that use cane juice or cane honey as their sugar source. This is because most, if not all, of the geographical and climactic influences that shape the material will be deadened during the sugar refinery process.

For those distillers that use cane juice as their base material (a practice popular in the French islands of the Caribbean) the variety of the cane, where it is grown, when it is harvested and how it is harvested are all scrutinized. The specific agriculture of the cane is often one of the major points of difference between distillers, discernible right through to the finished product. This begins with the variety of cane, where each type offers slightly different levels of sugar concentration (referred to as *Brix* and measured in ° Brix) and preferred growing conditions. Some varieties have been specifically bred or hybridized to be more disease-resistant, to thrive in volcanic soil, at higher altitudes or in hotter, low-lying regions. Others are prized more for their flavour, such as

B69-566 or "Blue Cane"– named after the colour of the yeast that naturally forms on it – which was originally bred in Barbados and now proudly features in various single-varietal release rums from Martinique and Guadeloupe.

There are other colours assigned to different cane varieties: red, green and blue. These colours do not always reflect in the appearance of the cane itself, though. Blue cane is more mauve in appearance, which the Martinican poet Patrick Chamoiseau seems to agree with when he described the "purple swathes of sugar cane [and] heady aroma of the first cane flowers."

Cane grown on higher ground, where humidity also tends to be higher, usually grows taller. This means it has a higher overall sugar content than low-grown canes, but the concentration of sugars is slightly lower. For the commercially minded rum manufacturer, higher concentrations of sugar are preferred, because this means more alcohol per ton of cane.

SUGARCANE PROCESSING

"You have to know how to cut the cane, talk to it as it falls, bundle it right away, take it to the grinders with due respect."
Patrick Chamoiseau, poet

Sugarcane is harvested during the dry season, which typically lands between January and July in the Caribbean and Latin America. Where possible, the cutting is done by machine, but it's still necessary to hand-cut the cane if the terrain is on a steep hillside, or generally impassable.

Cutting sugarcane by hand has to rank as one of the worst jobs on the planet. It's back-breaking, monotonous, hot and dangerous. I have tried my hand at it a number of times, and after only five minutes of cutting and stripping the cane with a machete, I was desperate to never cut another piece ever again.

On some plantations, where cane is cut by hand – and especially those in Latin America – the cane is first burned before it is harvested. While not an environmentally sound practice, this does make the hand-harvesting process a lot easier and reduces labour costs. The fire scorches the outside of the cane, which minimizes juice loss during cutting. It doesn't damage the main structure of the cane, but it does strip the cane of any dry pieces of fibre, and protects the dense grass from the attention of dangerous insects and snakes.

Where cane is cut by machines – usually by a sugarcane harvester, which was originally developed in the 1920s – it's usually conducted in tandem with a tractor trailer. The sugarcane harvester has a pair of conical shaped drills at the front that wind around, grabbing the cane and wrenching it from the earth. Underneath the cabin of the machine, the cane is chopped into smaller pieces in such a way that the extraction of juice is avoided and the green leaves are processed out of the mix. Less than a second has passed, and the cane pieces are now at the rear of the vehicle, where they are conveyed up, before being mercilessly tossed sideways into a trailer that's pulled along by a tractor.

Mechanical harvesting is only possible on flat or very nearly flat terrain, so the majority of the world's sugarcane is still cut by hand. Mechanical harvesting is more damaging to the cane itself compared with cut cane, and the farmer suffers greater harvest losses. It's also more ecologically damaging because it compacts soil and damages the root and stem of the remaining plant stub.

Quite recently there have been advances in smaller cane harvesters so they now look more like large lawnmowers. These machines aim to make the hand-harvesting process less gruelling in environments where large machines are impractical or unaffordable, and cause less damage to the environment.

However the cane has been cut, it's possible to encounter it being transported by any means imaginable. During the Caribbean harvesting seasons, roads and tracks are littered with dropped lengths of cane, which ideally needs pressing within 48 hours to prevent the sucrose being broken down into simpler sugars by the enzyme invertase.

Once the cane arrives at the mill, the crop is weighed and the value calculated. In some countries it is a legal requirement that a sample of cane is taken and the sugar content measured. Sweeter cane makes more alcohol, and is naturally worth more money, so this encourages farmers to cut it only when the plant has reached its peak ripeness. Once calculated, the sweetness and the weight are entered into a formula that gives a price that the farmer is paid.

In large sugar refineries and the biggest distilleries in Martinique and Guadeloupe, the cane is dumped onto large patios and pushed around by bulldozers that load it onto conveyor

LEFT The use of sugarcane harvesters, which were originally invented in the 1920s, certainly save a lot of time and effort, but they're no good on hillsides or on small plantations.

belts. In smaller distilleries, like River Antoine in Grenada, the canes can be bundled together and unloaded by hand.

MAKING SUGAR AND MOLASSES

Since most rums are made from molasses, which is a by-product of the sugar-refining process, it's useful to first understand how sugarcane is processed in the context of a modern sugar mill.

Once it has arrived at the mill, the sugarcane is fed into a series of conveyor belts and rolling cutters, which break and squash the cane into sequentially smaller pieces until all that's left is *bagasse* (pulp fibre) and free-running juice. The smell of these places is pungent – always sharply acidic like vinegar (indicating the constant presence of airborne yeast) – but also earthy, vegetal and of course sweet. Water is added during milling to help flush as much sucrose from the plant as possible.

Next, the heavy impurities from the raw cane juice are removed by a process of clarification, which sees a strong alkaline known as "milk of lime" (calcium hydroxide slurry) added to the juice. This neutralizes the acids, which prevents the sucrose from converting into starch. The lime slurry needs to be removed, however, so the juice is carbonated at high temperature, which converts the calcium hydroxide into calcium carbonate (limestone), which can easily be filtered out. Sulphur dioxide is added to the juice, which increases the acidity, lowering the juice from a pH of 9 to a pH of 5. It also bleaches the juice, helping to improve the flavour of the sugar and lightening the colour.

The next stage is concentration, where most of the water is evaporated from the juice, leaving behind a super-sweet syrup. This is performed in a low-pressure boiler (called a vacuum pan) which places the liquid under a partial vacuum as it is heated, lowering the boiling point, and avoiding the caramelization of the sugars in the juice.

Next comes crystallization, where the last portion of the water is evaporated under very strict controls. Seed grain (sugar granules) are fed into the vacuum pan and as the water evaporates, more crystals begin to form. This process is typically repeated three times, and each time the remaining syrup becomes darker and more viscous. After the third boil, the sugar crystals leave the vacuum pan as a thick brown snowball of sugar, at which point it is classed as muscovado sugar. This is then sent to a centrifuge for further refining into raw sugar of at least 96° Brix (the percentage of sugar by mass).

The syrup that is left in the pan is molasses, and is graded based on the number of times it has been boiled. The leftovers after the first boiling is known as "first syrup" or "light molasses". This has a relatively high sugar content and would typically be sent for further boiling, but it can be sold as "treacle" for baking. The remnants from the second boil are classed as "dark molasses" or "medium molasses" – it too can be used as a baking ingredient but one with far less purity and a good deal more colour. The remaining syrup from the third and final boil, when no more sugar can be liberated from the syrup, is "blackstrap molasses". It's not that there isn't any sugar left (blackstrap molasses from cane comprises roughly 30–40% sucrose and 20% other sugars) – it's just that it costs more money to extract the remaining sugar than the sugar itself is worth.

For the rum-maker, it's blackstrap that is of the most interest: just over half of all the rum distilleries in the Caribbean and Latin America (disregarding Haiti's 500-or-so distilleries that produce the fellow sugarcane spirit clairin) use blackstrap as their base material. But the distilleries using molasses are, on the whole, much bigger than the French island's *agricole* operations, so molasses-based rums account for over 90% of all the rum made in the Caribbean and Latin America. As black as boot polish, it's a viscous sludge that smells of liquorice (licorice) and iron and looks like congealed blood.

During cane sugar refining, no part of the cane is wasted. Once the juice is pressed, the *bagasse* is burnt. One ton of dry *bagasse* is equivalent in energy value to two barrels of fuel oil, and the heat it produces is used to create steam energy, which powers mills and pumps. Since fresh *bagasse* still contains around 50% water, it's usually dried on patios before being burned.

CANE HONEY

Cane honey is concentrated juice of the sugarcane plant. It's produced during the evaporation stage of the sugar- refining process and takes on the appearance of a thick honey-like syrup and is around 75° Brix. Cane honey intended for rum is usually made in much the same way as it is in a sugar mill (see earlier), only the process ends before the vacuum-pan stage, thus preventing crystallization of the sugar. When the rum-maker wishes to use the cane honey to make rum, they dilute the syrup with water, back down to around 20° Brix before fermentation.

Cane honey rums differ from those made from cane juice, because many of the volatile organic compounds that are present in the juice are lost during the evaporation process. This typically results in a fermentation with fewer congeners (substances other than alcohol produced during fermentation), which means far less of the banana and vegetal madness present in *agricole*-style rums. In truth,

LEFT Base materials for rum-making are available from this roadside seller in Grenada (if you can excuse their spelling).

cane honey rums are closer in style to molasses rums, but much of this depends on how conducive the fermentation and distillation processes are to retaining the character of the base material.

With the exception of St. Nicholas Abbey in Barbados, the distilleries that use cane honey to make their rums are all in Latin America (Guatemala, Panama and the Dominican Republic). And all of them run quite short fermentations and produce high-strength column-still distillates, so almost any trace of the cane honey flavour is lost. But even if these were pot-still rums, I think it's questionable whether – after a few years' maturation – you could pick out a cane honey rum among a selection of other molasses-based rums.

Rum producers that use cane honey tend to promote the flavour benefits, but the use of cane honey over molasses really boils down to economics. Whether it's taxes, subsidies, the price of sugar, price of molasses, or the cost of the labour force, sometimes it just makes better business sense to turn sugar cane into rum rather than sugar and molasses rum. These distilleries could of course just make cane juice spirits (in the *agricole* style), but cane syrup has the benefit of being a stable product. One that can be tucked away in a safe place and fermented long after the harvesting season has ended.

USING CANE JUICE IN RUM

Rums that are made from sugar cane juice rather than molasses, are most commonly referred to as *rhum agricole*. This is a French term, which translates to "agricultural rum" or "farm rum". In the past, the term *rhum agricole* usually referred to a small, self-sufficient type of producer rather than to the material that they made their rum from. Indeed, sugar cane juice rums were known as *rhum de vessou*, and cane syrup and molasses rums known as *rhum de syrup* and *rhum de melasse*.

Just as today's "craft" distilleries are keen to remind us of their relatively small operations, *rhum agricole* also spoke of boutique production and cottage industry. Larger operations, which tended to be in urban areas, and usually purchased their base material from a third party, were known as *rhum industriel* distilleries (see pages 77–78).

Rhum agricole rums begin their lives with similar mechanical processing as in sugar refineries – this isn't surprising, since many of them are a tribute to an old sugar mill. Once the cane is cut, the clock starts ticking and the race is on to mill the plant as quickly as possible to ensure maximum sugar – and therefore alcohol – yield. The cane is pressed, typically through a series of roller mills linked together by conveyor belts. In some distilleries, water is added at the time of pressing, and in the most modern examples, the quantity of water is adjusted by a computer in order to reach the optimum level of sweetness in the pressed juice. Foam and scum from the pressing, along with any debris/dirt or pieces of cane fibre, are filtered out of the juice, which is then sent for fermentation.

Cane juice rums are not to everyone's tastes. For me, there's a far stronger link to the plant and field with *rhum agricole* over those made from molasses and that's down to the fact that there are fewer stages of human intervention in the manufacturing process. Factors like cane variety, terroir and processing technique become highly relevant in this style, which opens up additional levels of distinction between similar products.

ABOVE Cane mills such as these are common to all *agricole* distilleries. This one is at Damoiseau distillery on Guadeloupe.

As Dave Broom puts it in *Rum* (2003): "it's somehow appropriate that the French make rum in this fashion as, in many ways, it is one step closer to wine."

FERMENTATION

Fermentation is an essential stage of the rum-making process because it is here where all the alcohol is made! Through the action of millions of yeast cells, alcohol molecules are manufactured from the sugars present in molasses or sugarcane juice/syrup. But fermentation is also a crucial stage in the development of flavour in a rum – that is, if the rum you're making is to be flavourful. There are many factors at play during fermentation, some of them easier to control than others, but the key variables here are the type of yeast that is used and the length of the fermentation.

These days, most distilleries use a distiller's yeast to ferment their molasses or cane products. This will be a specific strain of the fast-acting yeast *Saccharomyces cerevisiae* – the same species that has been used by brewers and breadmakers since ancient times. The type of yeast used will not only affect the

yield of alcohol, but can also control the rate and intensity of fermentation, and ultimately the complex flavourful congeners that are created. Distiller's yeasts offer the most efficient rate of conversion, but often do so at the cost of flavour. Some distilleries use proprietary yeast strains that aim to produce specific flavours during fermentation.

Yeast can be added to the fermenting vessel in one of two ways, either by tipping 20-kg (44-lb) bags of living culture in by hand, or by pumping liquid yeast in through pipes. Some more modern distilleries use yeast propagation tanks, which provide optimal conditions for yeast cell cultures to multiply before further sugars are added. Some more traditional rum distillers don't add a yeast culture at all, instead allowing natural airborne yeasts to let fermentation work its magic.

If the distillery is making rum from cane juice, it's a ready-made source of sugar and ready to be fermented straight out of the cane. In the case of molasses and cane juice, these products are too dense to be fermented as they are – which is also the reason why they constitute a "shelf-stable" product (i.e. one that can be stored safely at room temperature) – so they must be diluted with water first. A distillery may also add a yeast nutrient to the molasses, which helps to promote a healthy fermentation. This typically takes the form of ammonium sulphate, which helps to boost nitrogen levels and keep the yeast active.

When a yeast is exposed to a sugary environment in the tropics, it gets to work in less than an hour. Fermentation begins with the metabolic process called glycolysis, where yeast converts one glucose (sugar) molecule into two pyruvate molecules. Pyruvate is a form of "free energy" that can be used to create other energy-providing compounds, and this is exactly the same process that takes place in the human body to convert glucose into a usable energy currency.

Pyruvate features three carbon atoms. During the fermentation of bread, it is these atoms that combine with the yeast and oxygen to make carbon dioxide (CO_2). Voilà: your bread proves. In the case of fermenting sugary liquids, such as molasses and cane juice, the liquid doesn't have access to much oxygen – a layer of CO_2 sits on top of the brew, and oxygen can't penetrate down through the liquid. This lack of oxygen means that the process is described as "anaerobic". In this instance the pyruvate can't combine all its carbon with oxygen (to create CO_2), so it instead produces molecules of ethanol, methanol and other types of alcohol.

Heat can become problematic in the hot environments in which rum distilleries traditionally locate themselves, and if the temperature of the fermentation rises above 38°C (100°F), there is a chance that the yeast cells will die in a kind of hot soup of their own making. It's for this reason that some distilleries run liquid-cooling lines through their fermenters, to cool things down a little. In non-traditional rum-producing regions, the problem is flipped on its head, and sometimes it's necessary to warm the fermentation vessels gently to promote yeast culture growth and encourage fermentation.

It is the ethanol that gives the fermented liquid its alcoholic strength,

but the other alcohols produced, along with development of aldehydes and esters, are the true designators of flavour. The variety and quantity of these compounds is dictated by a whole number of factors that are not limited to the mineral content and pH of the cane juice or the syrup/molasses and any added water; the length and temperature of fermentation and the type of yeast used are also key factors.

Longer fermentation is the most significant of these factors, as highlighted by the 30-day "flavour-makers" (i.e. the month-long process of fermentation) that take place at distilleries like Hampden Estate in Jamaica. These rums owe much of their flavour and aroma to complex organic compounds called esters, which are generated during longer fermentations when acids in the wash/wine react with alcohols. The acids themselves are created by the secondary fermentation of alcohols, and by the action of *lactobacillus* bacteria on residual

RIGHT Fermentation tanks at La Favorite on the island of Martinique. Nitrogen and phosphate are sometimes added as nutrients for yeast, and the fermentation may also be acidified to prevent bacterial contamination.

sugars. Esters are also created by the organic reduction of aldehydes that are themselves created by the oxidation of alcohol. Low-molecular-weight esters are present in many natural fruits, herbs and flowers, and it's these compounds that give us the suggestion of fruitiness or floral aroma in rum. More esters are produced in longer fermentation (at the sacrifice of alcohol content) as the alcoholic wash/wine is given an extended opportunity to oxidize and reduce.

A lighter style of rum needs only a short fermentation (typically 18–48 hours, because the product is intended to be light in flavour). Heavier rums tend to be fermented for as much as five days – we'll explore distilleries' approaches to this in The Rum Tour chapter.

The final strength of the fermented wash/wine will vary according to many of the factors listed above, not least of all the sugar content (Brix) of the starting wort. In general though, wash/wine strength will sit somewhere between 5 and 8%, so something like a strong beer.

MUCK AND DUNDER

Some Jamaican distilleries undergo a process known as "dundering" during fermentation, which is similar to that of sour-mashing in the Bourbon industry. However, with Bourbon it's a simple case of adding leftover acidic stillage (or *vinasse*) to the ferment, whereas with dunder there's a little more to it… and it isn't pretty.

A "dunder pit" is where this magic/ horror takes place. In this pit, the waste stillage is mixed with cane vinegar, fresh molasses and water, and the whole horrific mess is aerated over a period of hours. The precise cocktail of ingredients is designed to create the perfect breeding ground for bacteria, and this oozing mass

of infected goo is affectionately referred to as "muck". As the bacteria multiply, they produce a range of long-chain fatty (carboxylic) acids, each of which will come in handy during fermentation when they react with alcohol to create esters. The resulting aromas are funky beyond all measure, like defiled fruit. Aficionados of the style call it "hogo", which is derived from the French term *haut gout* (good flavour), a term that also lends itself to that most infamous affliction of the gourmand – gout.

There are many historical references to "muck holes" from the early 20th century, during a time when high-ester Jamaican rums were sought-after ingredients for culinary applications such as in candy production. The muck hole operates like a bioreactor with the aim of creating nice, complex carboxylic acids. The problem is that, if left unchecked, the muck becomes overly acidic, resulting in the production of ammonia, before finally stalling. This is managed by adding the alkaline lime marl (crumbly sedimentary rock comprising limestone and clay), which keeps the pH in check and helps create acid crystals/salts which could be drawn off as fresh stillage was added. Cane vinegar is added because it's made from acetic acid. This is good from a flavour standpoint as – being the shortest chain acid – it readily bonds with lime marl to form salt crystals. Acetic acid trades places with longer-chain acids, and allows them to partake in the creation of more interesting aroma-giving esters.

POT DISTILLATION

Pot stills are the simplest and oldest form of distillation. They work like large kettles: an alcoholic wash/wine is heated, the vapours are channelled up to the top

ABOVE A beguiling, if not just downright confusing, dunder chart at Hampden Estate. I hope it makes more sense to them than it does to me.

(neck) of the still and then into the condenser where they are converted back into a liquid. Pot stills are usually made from copper, which is used because of its high thermal conductivity, malleability and catalytic properties.

Distillation in pots is quite inefficient, however, and distillation runs are often repeated in a batch process to increase alcohol strength. Logic would suggest that any alcoholic liquid that is heated should produce a vapour of 100% pure alcohol, but some water inevitably finds itself into each distillation because water vapour and steam are generated even at very low temperatures.

In a traditional pot still, the first distillation only produces a "spirit" of around 25–30% alcohol by volume (ABV). The second distillation results in a liquid of typically 65–75% ABV – sufficient in strength to be called a spirit. It's possible to distil this spirit a third time – although I know of no rums that

do so – but there is little advantage in doing this, as the crudeness of the process limits the potential concentration of alcohol.

It's not just alcohol that carries through in pot distillation. As the wash/wine is heated from the bottom, the system generates upward pressure that forces alcohol and water precipitates, as well as volatile aromatic molecules (but not colour) up through the neck of the still, along the lyne arm and down into the condenser. Taller stills produce a lighter style of spirit, because they make it harder for heavier compounds to make the journey uphill. Short stills encourage the transfer of heavier compounds into the condenser, making a rum style with greater depth and lingering flavour.

Tall stills give a spirit more interaction time (and space) with copper. Copper has a purifying effect on a distilled spirit, and a greater degree of interaction removes sulphurous flavours and heightens the cultivation of delicate fruit and floral aromatics. This is especially so in small stills, since there is a greater surface area of copper in relation to the volume of liquid. Of course, the effects of size vary based on how much liquid is put in the still too. The shape of the still also has a part to play, with the different forms encouraging a varying degree of reflux in the system. A short still can produce spirit that is reminiscent of a tall still by bulging out and pinching in at certain stages up the neck of the still.

Modern stills are powered by steam coils or steam jackets, but older examples can be directly fired by an oil or gas flame or by burning wood or *bagasse*. Direct firing is thought to produce a spirit heavier in character, as hot spots on the inside of the still burn the wash/wine (and especially any insoluble matter contained in it) causing complex caramelizations, Maillard reactions, charring of solid matter and the production of furfural (an oily liquid with an almond-like aroma) and sulphur compounds that may carry through into the final product.

Whatever the style of rum, it's always necessary to "cut" the freshly distilled spirit during the second distillation to remove dangerous and unpleasant smelling compounds. The first cut is known as the "heads" and contains higher alcohols and ketones, which besides being toxic also give the spirit the aroma of glue or turpentine. The heads typically represent the first 5% of a complete run, and after collection they are sometimes redistilled in the next batch to liberate any remaining ethanol. Next the main body of the spirit (known as the "heart") begins to flow from the condenser – this is effectively high-strength white rum. Finally, towards the end of the run, it's necessary to make a second cut, as the "tails" begin to come through. These comprise heavier, oily alcohols that can give a spirit a rough and unclean flavour, as well as making it cloudy in appearance. Again, some distilleries will redistill a portion of the tails too.

The exact cut of the "heart" differs according to the distiller's preference, with every subsequent litre of distillate highlighting specific characteristics generated during fermentation – from light florals, to citrus freshness, down to vibrant berries and rich, dark fruits.

RETORT IS THE ANSWER

In the world of rum, pot stills rarely operate in isolation. Most have a pair of "retorts"connected between the lyne arm and the condenser. A retort is like an additional, smaller pot that conducts a further distillation of the spirit vapour,

ABOVE Pot stills – like those at Mount Gay (top) and St. Lucia Distillers (above) – are the backbone of the world's best blended rums.

increasing the strength and removing the need to run a second "batch" distillation.

The pot is filled with alcoholic wash/wine as normal, which is heated until the vapour (of around 30% ABV) is carried over into the first retort. Here it is met by "low wines" from the previous distillation, which mix with the vapour and boil, doubling the spirit vapour strength up to roughly 60% ABV. This vapour carries over into the next retort, which contains the "high wines" from the previous distillation. The spirit vapour once again increases in strength, this time up to 88% ABV, and then passes into the condenser. The liquid that flows off is then cut four ways: heads, heart (rum), high wines and low wines, where the latter two are recycled back into the retorts ready for the next distillation.

COLUMN DISTILLATION

The important distinction to make between pot stills and column stills is the concept of a "batch" process. In pot distillation, the efficiency of the distillation and the character of the resulting liquid is orchestrated by duration of the distillation and the timing of the cuts – it is an artisanal process requiring both technical training and an understanding of the organoleptic properties of the spirit. A column still is different. It's a continuous process that need never end so long as there is a good supply of alcoholic liquid fed into the system, and it's for this reason that the column still is sometimes referred to as a "continuous still". But there is a common misconception that all column stills are the same, and that they all produce the same, largely neutral, industrial spirit. This is an unfair assessment, however. Generally speaking, the more columns in a continuous still setup, the purer – or to put it another way, "neutral" – the resulting spirit becomes.

Column stills seem like quite modern innovations, but they have been around since the 1830s and early versions were being developed 200 years before then. One of the first continuous stills was invented by Frenchman Edouard Adam, who attended chemistry lectures under Professor Laurent Solimani at the University of Montpellier. Amazingly, Adam was illiterate, but despite that

apparently minor setback, he developed and patented the first type of column still in 1804. Unrecognizable from the stills you can see on page 62, Adam's column was a horizontal arrangement that linked together a series of "large eggs", with pipes that routed alcohol vapour from one egg to the next. The strength of the spirit increased in each subsequent egg, whilst the leftover stuff was recycled back at the start again.

The Pistorius still, which was patented in 1817, was the first still to be arranged in a column shape. Steam was pumped up from the bottom and beer from the top and distillation took place on a series of perforated "plates" arranged through the length of the column. This design worked best because it allowed for a smooth graduation of temperature change from higher at the bottom to lower at the top. Since ethyl alcohol boiled at exactly 78.3°C (172.9°F), in theory you could fraction spirit vapour off the column at a height that corresponded to that temperature and capture a very high-strength spirit, leaving most of the (undesirable) residual flavour behind.

Subsequent iterations were developed in France and Scotland, and by 1830 the final design had been settled upon, fully realized in a design patented by the Inspector General of Excise in Ireland, Aeneas Coffey. The "Coffey Still" or "Patent Still" was a truly continuous process, where fermented beer (or wine) was pumped in and high-strength alcohol drawn off. It was even quite energy-efficient for its time, using the cool pipes that fed beer into the system as condensing coils for the hot alochol vapours exiting it – like a dog eating its own tail.

In Coffey's design, two columns are at work, with both of them separated into

chambers by a series of perforated plates. Starting in the rectifying column, the wash/wine is carried down through a coiled pipe and heated as it goes. The wash/wine is then pumped up to the top of the analyzer column, where it is sprayed on to the top plate, and falls through the holes, gradually making its way to the bottom. At the bottom of the analyser, steam is pumped into the system, which rises up to meet the falling wash/wine. This has the effect of stripping the alcohol from the wash/wine, which then rises back up the analyzer; it is then pumped out (owing to the pressure) before travelling down to the base of the rectifier. Once there, it continues to evaporate upwards, with each plate acting like a single distillation run. As it nears the top, it begins to cool, because only the lightest part of the vapour can continue upwards. Once it reaches the collecting plate (which is set by the distiller) the spirit is allowed to flow out, fully concentrated and up to 95% pure alcohol.

The number of plates in the two columns dictates the final strength of the spirit: fewer plates produce a more characterful, less refined liquid. More plates, more columns, and taller columns result in a purer style of distillate, but it also means a greater degree of flexibility in the style of distillate that is produced, as different combinations of columns are connected or removed from the sequence. Most Latin American distilleries operate entirely with columns, often producing different weights of marque that can be used in a final blend.

HYBRID STILLS

Although hybrid stills seem like relatively new innovations, they have their origins in much older distilleries. Some of the first column stills on Puerto Rico and Cuba were in fact hybrids – pot stills with columns mounted on top. These days, a hybrid still usually looks like a pot still with a column connected on the side. By opening and closing the plates on the column, the distiller can select how heavy or light the rum comes off the still.

MATURATION

Ask someone to picture "rum" in their head, and it's quite likely they will think of an oak barrel. Barrels or casks are linked to rum's history, just as they are to its flavour. Since its earliest conception in the 17th century, rum has been shifted around in barrels, from island to mainland, from sugar mill to port, from distillery to blender. Before the dawn of of the forklift truck and pallet, the oak barrel was the trustiest of vessels to store your goods. It's been around since Roman times, and for some 2,000 years it has been the go-to method of transportation for pretty much everything – be it fish, nails, coins, booze, or dead admirals (in the case of Admiral Horatio Nelson): the unique shape of a wooden barrel – that pinches inwardly at both ends – makes it surprisingly easy for a single person to move hundreds of kilograms of cargo around by themselves. Barrels are watertight, relatively cheap to "raise", highly durable (some last over a century before being decommissioned) and easy to store. The unique nature of wood as a storage material also means that air and vapours can move freely in and out of the cask, while the liquid stays safe inside. This is a key element of the maturation process. Best of all, though – they can turn fiery white rum into a spirit of nuance and distinction.

TYPES OF OAK

To better understand how oak affects a white rum, we must get to grips with the material itself.

Most of the barrels in the spirits industry are made in the US and intended for the production of Bourbon whiskey, or constructed in Spain and France, where they are used to age sherry, wines, and brandy. The rest of the

ABOVE Hybrid German stills are very popular with gin distillers, and we're starting to see them used to make rum too.

spirits-producing world (including rum, Scotch, and Tequila) purchases second-hand barrels from these producers in the US, Spain and France in order to age their products. This system of *build, use, sell, use,* is born out the economics of availability and the trading patterns that were established centuries ago. But the use of new barrels in the Bourbon and Cognac industries has in turn defined the style of those spirits, with their up-front, concentrated, oak characteristics.

Bourbon casks make up the vast majority of the barrels used by the rum industry and are made from a variety of oak known as "white oak" (*Quercus alba*). This type of oak has a paler-coloured bark than other varieties, although the colour of the cut wood is indistinguishable from any other. White oak is a fast-growing variety, rising straight and true and reaching maturation in only 60–80 years. The result is wood influence that we commonly associate with rum: plenty of vanilla and other associated "white" things, such as banana, white chocolate, buttermilk and custard.

White oak casks are built in the US, filled with Bourbon, emptied and then sold to rum makers. US law prohibits the refilling of these casks, so Bourbon producers are legally obliged to move them on to other industries. Second-hand goods they may be, but having been stripped of some of their flavour, they are less aggressive in their delivery of wood characteristics and easier to control than new casks – think of it like a tea bag that, after brewing a cup, still has plenty of flavour to give to a second, third, or even fourth cup… if left to brew for long enough.

European oak casks are generally used and sold in much the same way as Bourbon casks are: filled one or more times, then sold on to other industries. European oak casks can be made from white oak or red oak (*Quercus robur*) which is a slower growing tree, that twists and turns and only reaches maturation after 150 years. The resulting spirit tends to be more tannic (a trait of the slow growth), peppery and spicy with, rather fittingly, flavours of red-coloured things like dried plums, grapes, cloves and red wine. The wine or brandy

that previously filled the cask will have stripped some of the flavour out (just as Bourbon does) but the cask still has plenty left to give, as well as some residual flavours from the wine (or spirit) that it previously contained. Ex-wine and sherry casks are prized by the Scotch whisky industry, but have made little headway into the rum world. Distillers such as Foursquare in Barbados, Brugal in the Dominican Republic and St Lucia Distillers in St Lucia are among the pioneers of these new premium offerings – more to come in the future, I hope.

In the French-speaking islands of the Caribbean, it's quite common to encounter French oak casks, made from *Quercus sessliflora* that grows in the Limousin Forest. These have often passed through the Cognac industry first, but in certain distilleries, like Barbancourt in Haiti, it's the new cask that's used. These casks offer up zestiness, spice and plenty of grippy tannin.

New American oak casks are rare to find in rum distilleries, although some producers are experimenting with them on a small scale, curious to find out what a new-oak cask can contribute to a rum blend.

CHARRING AND TOASTING

Whatever the type of oak, the barrel will be charred (in Bourbon barrel production) or toasted (in European oak barrel production) at the time of its construction, and possibly again, later in its life. The origins of this practice are not entirely clear, but some historians suggest that it was a means of removing the taint of the product that the barrel previously held (fish, for example) before filling it with

LEFT Although any type of barrel can be used to age rum, the most common varieties are French and American oak.

wine or spirit. Bourbon's alleged inventor, Reverend Elijah Craig, is sometimes credited as the originator of the practice. That's also an alleged claim.

Charring is an all-out flamethrower assault in the interior surfaces of the barrel, as ruthless licks of heat blast the wood for 30–60 seconds, causing the surface to bubble and writhe as it catches fire. When a cask is toasted, the heat is applied more gently, sometimes through convection rather than direct flame, and over a longer period of time – up to and around 6 minutes. Think of it like frying versus baking. Baking the barrels like this results in the degradation of wood polymers into flavoursome compounds, the destruction of unpleasant resinous compounds in the wood, and in the case of charring, the forming of a thin layer of active carbon. The two different approaches also play to the flavour palates of the associated spirit industries.

THE MATURATION MECHANISM

Ageing rum is not as simple as "the longer you leave it the more woody it gets", and certainly not as simple as "the older the rum the better it tastes". An age statement on a bottle can be useful, but it only really becomes relevant if the other variables are made

aware to us: the type and condition of wood, age of the cask, how many times it has been filled and various environmental factors.

Newer casks will give a rum more flavour, and it's for this reason that you may encounter an amber-coloured 3-year-old next to a straw-coloured 10-year-old (using the same teabag three or four times will produce similar results). That's not to say that refill casks are worthless, in fact it's sometimes a more pleasantly subdued and considered flavour that we find from these older barrels.

Much of what goes on in the perpetual twilight of a warehouse, however, is unpredictable without the analysis of every stave of wood that makes up every cask and every drop of liquid that goes into it. The changes that take effect in the murky realms of the vessel are, even today, still being scrutinized and tested to better understand the effects of the barrel and the optimum maturation conditions.

We're not completely in the dark though. Oak itself contains over 100 volatile components capable of contributing flavour in a rum. Additionally there are other compounds formed through the oxidation of wood extracts and compounds already present in the freshly made spirit. It's these factors that broadly affect the flavour of an aged spirit.

Looking at this in more detail, there are four components of oak structure that contribute flavour to rum: lignin, hemicellulose, extractives and oak tannins. Once charred or toasted, the lignin in the oak contributes to flavours of toast, coffee, vanilla and then caramel, chocolate, toffee and cream.

Hemicellulose is the breeze block of oak's secondary cell walls. It is thought to react with complex acids in the spirit, causing simple un-sweet wood sugars (around 200 different types) to be extracted that provide body and "smoothness" to the liquid. Extractives are free-running solubles that get washed out by the rum. They include a whole host of flavour compounds that can provide grassy, baked, wood-sap, peachy, floral and even greasy aromas. Wood tannin gives the familiar drying sensation on the palate, and when managed correctly, balance and grip to an otherwise flabby spirit. Tannins also impart colour and astringent flavour, at least in the early phase of maturation, and take part in various oxidative reactions removing sulphury off-notes and promoting colour stability, lignin breakdown and oxidation of alcohol into acetals, producing ethereal top-notes.

Last, but certainly not least, is the chemical degradation of the liquid through oxidation. Besides ethanol, there are numerous other trace alcohols present in rum, each with its own weight and flavour and each capable of being turned into aldehydes and acids. For example, the oxidation of the ethanol (alcohol) in the cask forms acetaldehyde and acetic acid. Aldehydes play an important role in rum aroma, like benzaldehyde (oxidized benzyl alcohol), which smells like almond.

Acetic acid, along with other oxoacids are crucial for the formation of esters. Esters provide all of the fruity and floral top notes in rum aroma, everything from geranium or jasmine right through to apple, sage, pineapple and strawberry.

CLIMATIC CONSIDERATIONS

Climate affects rum at virtually every stage of production, from the cane to fast ferments and accelerated maturation.

Casks are organic containers, each one like a wooden lung that "breathes" in its immediate environment through the course of the day. Alcohol and water are in a constant state of evaporation, and they both move out of the cask, making way for the incoming air. The hotter the climate and the greater the variance between day and night, the faster this process occurs. Over time, the volume of the cask depreciates and the liquid dissipates, and in the tropics this occurs at a rate of 5% to 10% of the total contents of the barrel every year. In particularly hot climates, like Venezuela and Guyana, a distillery might expect to lose half of the barrel in the space of five years.

On some French-speaking islands, *rhum agricole* producers "top-up" casks with similar-aged rum as the level in the barrel drops. This physical intervention

LEFT These vertically-oriented barrels at Brugal in the Dominican Republic are typically aged for 1–3 years.

in the maturation process is known as *élevage* ("breeding"). It's a canny way of reducing the number of casks that the distillery needs to store, but it also reduces the angel's share and affects the flavour of the future rum by minimizing oxidative reactions.

I have heard it said that spirits aged in the tropics mature five or ten times faster (depending on who you speak to) than in the chilly climes of the whisky or Cognac industries. But I think that statements like these can be a little misleading and are founded upon unscientific principles. Certainly, the interactive effect of the oak is accelerated, as the contraction and expansion of the cask is amplified by hot days and cool nights. This is why the spirit colours so quickly, as tannins are quickly drawn out of the cask. Evaporative losses are much higher in the Caribbean, so the spirit concentrates much faster, and this also has the apparent effect of speeding up maturation. The increased headspace in the cask (as the liquid evaporates) also increases the rate of oxidation, because when the cask empties, the area of exposed liquid increases until the cask is half full. But the increase in surface area alone is enough for a five-fold increase in oxidative degradation.

So in some respects the maturation is accelerated significantly, and in others it is but a slight change. The point is, that a rum matured for five years in the Caribbean and a rum matured for 15 years in France, will not taste the same. Climactic considerations have too great an influence here for us to be able to compare one age statement to another, even if the starting liquid and cask are identical. The fact that even subtle shifts in temperature, air pressure and humidity can affect rum quite dramatically is

ABOVE Deciphering the complex nature of spirits maturation is a skill that took decades to master.

certainly something to be celebrated, and comes as no surprise for a product born out of such humble origins as cane and wood.

SOLERA AGEING

The process of solera ageing has its origins in the production of sherry, so it's not surprising that it should find its home in some of the Spanish-speaking distilleries in the West Indies, and it's brands like Santa Teresa and Zacapa that have found the most fame in this particular field.

A solera traditionally comprises three or four horizontal "layers" of casks, which are all filled with rums of the same average age. Rum for bottling is vatted from liquid drawn from the casks on the bottom layer, nearest the ground ("suelo" means "ground" in Spanish, which is where the term "solera" is taken from) but these casks are never completely emptied. The bottom layer is then topped up with rum from the second layer, which is topped up from the next layer, and so on. The top layer is topped up with other aged stocks from outside of the system, or with white rum.

Solera is a system of both maturation

and blending that maintains consistency and balances old with new and the rum drawn from the solera system will contain some small percentage of rum that is as old as the system itself. Well, that's how the system is supposed to work, anyway.

In reality, it isn't always practical to store barrels in layers on top of one another. The "layers" may constitute entire warehouses, where the rum is vatted in between each step. With some distilleries, the term "solera" has only vague similarities to the sherry-making process, such as with Ron Zacapa's incredibly convoluted *sistema solera*, which mixes static ageing, the French practice of *élevage* (see page 69) and some elements of Spanish solera all into one system.

BLENDING

Blending is nigh-on impossible to avoid in the world of rum. Almost all rums are blended in some shape or form: a blending of casks, ages, distillates or distilleries. Blending balances flavour, defines a product's style, and hedges bets, like an insurance policy against the possibility of certain rums becoming unavailable, if you will. It also stretches volumes, lengthening flavoursome heavy rum with lighter-style spirit. Imagine a finished bottle of rum like a piece of music, where all of the component parts form a harmonious balance of flavour. Sometimes it's nice to experience an unblended rum – a solo piece – but for the most part we are looking for balance and synergy. In this analogy, different styles of rum are representative of different musical instruments – from the bass notes of Demerara or Jamaica, to the high-pitched treble of column-still Spanish rums. Orchestrating these

separate components into a finished composition – whether from the same distillery or not – is where the artistry of the blender comes into play.

Further difficulty arises when re-creating that composition time and time again. In an orchestra you would find the best musicians of their time to play the piece, but as any concert-goer knows, there will always be subtle changes to the arrangement in each subsequent portrayal. The blender (or conductor) has similar challenges in the form of changes in distillery character and – if the rum is aged – price and availability of casks.

Practically speaking, the master blender will nose and taste cask samples, then compose a blend based on his or her findings. The distillery staff will then be tasked with dumping the liquid from all the relevant casks and mixing the liquid together in stainless steel tanks or occasionally large wooden vats.

FILTERING

All rum undergoes some degree of filtration, through steel, cellulose or nylon mesh, to remove particles attracted during the distillation process, or from time spent in cask.

Some rums are also chill-filtered. This process is the same as any other mechanical filtration method, except the spirit is chilled to approximately 0°C (32°F) (and sometimes much lower) prior to filtration. The chilling is necessary to draw certain fatty-acids and long-chain esters out of solution, which would turn the liquid cloudy if it is subjected to particularly cold (sub-zero) storage conditions, or if served over ice or from the freezer. While this is thought to only subtly change the flavour of the spirit, it would appear to be an acceptable compromise for a brand that doesn't wish to have their liquid turn cloudy on store shelves. Not everyone agrees that chill-filtering has a positive impact on quality, however. Some rum producers are beginning to follow the lead of the Scotch whisky industry and labelling their product as non-chill filtered – their belief being that process diminishes mouthfeel and removes precious flavour-giving components from the rum.

Cloudiness can also be a sign of a potentially dangerous product, but assuming you are assured of the provenance of the bottles, it's nothing to worry about.

Some rums, especially those of Spanish origin, may be filtered through charcoal prior to blending and bottling. This process is intended to soften flavour, but also to remove colour. Bacardí Carta Blanca is perhaps the best example of such a rum, as this spirit is matured for around two years, yet in the bottle it is crystal clear. The process also irons out discrepancies in colour, in some respects achieving the same effect as adding distiller's caramel but by removing colour instead.

Activated charcoal is a type of carbon that has been treated with oxygen. These lightweight black granules are unique and unrivalled in their surface area-to-mass ratio – a single gram can have a surface area in excess of 500 square meters! The more surface, the better the chance that large impure molecules adsorb onto the mass of the charcoal; activated charcoal can adsorb up to 20 times its weight. This can be a good or bad thing, since charcoal is not great at discriminating between "bad" and "good" flavour molecules. Either way, it's been used in spirits production for over two centuries, and is especially important for vodka, where flavour-free is often the goal.

SWEETENING

Although rum is inextricably linked with sugar, and many rums do indeed smell of "sweet" things (honey, toffee, treacle, etc.), rum will never taste truly sweet unless it has been sweetened before bottling. Virtually all of the sugars provided by molasses or cane juice are converted into alcohol during fermentation, and any residual sugars that are left behind do not carry over

LEFT Diversifying the flavour of rum stocks is the best way for a master blender to compose a balanced product.

ABOVE Testing the organoleptic properties of some cask samples in the lab at St. Lucia Distillers.

flavour and flatten nuance.

Most distillers that admit to adding sugar claim to do so because they are trying to iron out discrepancies in flavour from batch to batch. In other words: to ensure consistency. I'm fine with this – it's something that's practised in other spirit categories besides rum, most notably in the Cognac business, which refers to the sweetening of their liquids with the innocent sounding term "dosage". With Cognac, the legal limit is 2 g of sugar per litre of spirit – a barely detectable quantity.

But what is more frustrating than the act of sweetening itself, is the reluctance of distilleries to own up to it. "Do you add sugar?" is a question I often ask when touring distilleries, and it's often followed by a period of awkward silence. The producers that do add only a little (less than 5 g/litre) are usually quite honest about doing so. Conversely, it's the rums that are noticeably sweet (I'm looking at you, Central America and Guyana) that are keeping tight-lipped. Transparency has never been more sought-after in food and drink than it is today, both for the health conscious seeking assurances and for those interested in provenance and the integrity of manufacturing.

In 2014 the government-owned Swedish liquor store chain Systembolaget, and Alko, a similar chain of stores in Finland, ran a series of tests on a range of over 30 popular rum brands. The products were mostly from Spanish-speaking islands in the Caribbean, and Central and South American countries. Their results were, for the most part, quite consistent, and both studies made for a rather disturbing read. At the lower end of the scale, the younger island rums, such as Havana Club, Brugal and Bacardi, contained around 3 g sugar per litre of spirit. At the higher end there

during distillation. And it's because of this fact that rum bottled fresh from the still will have no sugar in it whatsoever. Even barrels, with all their associated caramels and vanilla contribute only trace quantities of actual sugar.

With that in mind, it may be surprising to learn that many popular rums do contain sugar and therefore have been sweetened. This goes for white rums as well as darker expressions, although it is in the latter that we tend to find the most liberal use of sweetener. This is nothing new – sugar has been added to rum for centuries – which is hardly surprising given the availability of the stuff in and around rum distilleries. Sweetening rum has the effect of softening alcohol burn and highlighting selected characteristics, as well as thickening the texture and the apparent concentration of the liquor. And it's for this reason – to make the rum more approachable – that sweetening has become an industry-wide practice. The problem is, some rums are so sweet that they are in danger of approaching a liqueur level of sweetness, and in my opinion, too much sugar can also muddy were some rums, like Ron Zacapa 23, Diplomatico Reserva Exclusiva, and Rhum Quorhum Solera 23 that each contained over 40 g sugar per litre of spirit. These figures are difficult to discredit, since testing was rigorous and conducted by two independent bodies.

Some of these producers still insist that the sugar in their rum comes from the barrel or from some proprietary production technique, relating to still shape or fermentation procedure.

The issue lies in the fact that adding sugar to rum, just like adding colour, is unregulated. Producers can choose to sweeten as they wish, and it's consumers that will make the final decision with their wallets on whether the rum is enjoyable or not. I personally think that some sweet rums are really rather delicious, but that certainly doesn't mean that good rum has to be sweetened aggressively, or that an amazing rum need have any sugar adding to it at all.

It's unlikely we will see an end to sugaring in rum, and I'm not sure that it needs to stop. What would be nice though, is some transparency on the matter. Labelling that clearly defines how much sugar has been added to the rum. With that information we can better understand why we like certain rums, and how we assign value to that.

COLOURING

Colouring is common among many aged (and some of the un-aged) rums. In fact, it's common among almost all spirits, as a means of standardizing the appearance of bottles on the liquor store shelf, and suggesting a little more time in oak than the natural spirit's colour might communicate.

This is achieved using distiller's caramel (E150a), which is obtained through the heating and caramelization of carbohydrates (sugar). So, it is in fact, just caramel. E150a has no sweetness to it however, since the process is carefully controlled so as to caramelize all of the available sugars, resulting in a very thick, black syrup. By itself the flavour is bitter, if anything, and a little goes a very long way. A pinprick of caramel is enough to muddy a sink-full of water.

Judging the rum by its colour is futile at the best of times, but once the element of colouring is introduced, the relationship between the colour of the liquid, its time spent in oak and the flavour one might expect of the liquid, is misleading to say the least. In fact, it's designed to fool you. The practice of adding colour to suggest long years in casks is one of the longstanding hallmarks of the Black Rum style. The irony being that, while these rums may appear to be long in years, they are generally a blend of either very young or even un-aged spirits. Mutton dressed as lamb, you might say.

Think about it enough (as I have) and it eventually leads one to question whether the colouring of rum really matters at all. Scientific studies on this subject suggest that the associated flavours of oak are perceptible in both spirits that are aged in oak and those that only appear to have been. It's a great example of how the colour of a drink can have profound influences on our perception of its flavour: "eye appeal is half the meal", so the saying goes. Take a nose on a glass of Navy rum and it's difficult to stifle similarly coloured flavour descriptors like "oak", "toffee", "molasses", "coffee" and "spice". The same rum without any adulteration of colour would not attract the same vocabulary. Ignorance is bliss. At the end

LEFT It's easy to dismiss colouring as cheating, but most of us struggle to disassociate dark spirits with quality.

of the day we are only fooling ourselves though, and blenders have been perfecting this art for at least two centuries.

RUM CLASSIFICATION

The single greatest challenge that rum faces in the 21st century is how it should be labelled. Whisky has its single malts and blends, brandy has age designations by VS, VSOP and XO. Even that most abused of spirits, Tequila, has strict classification terms that make it a relatively easy category to navigate around. Rum has never had an effective system of classification, and it's certainly about time it did.

The problem stems from the fact that there are no universal regulations concerning how rum should be labelled. Rum is made across five continents and in as many as 50 countries, many of which have their own regulations and rules regarding how the liquid is produced and how long it is aged for. Getting them all to agree on an overarching labelling policy is simply not going to happen.

So we make up our own rules around classification, as a means of communicating rum style and finding some orderliness amongst all the confusion.

In the past, many of us have communicated rum style in colours: white, light, silver, blanca, gold, oro, dark etc. But basing flavour on colour alone is an ill-defined and often misleading way of communicating rum flavour. Many budget "gold" or "dark" rums are in fact un-aged or very young rums that get much of their colour from caramel colouring, while some rums that are aged in barrels are filtered to remove their colour. These production elements are poorly legislated at best, and open to blatant abuse at worst, so they skew the whole system, creating broader misunderstanding of rum in general, which in turn makes it a difficult category of spirits to engage with.

More recently, we have found a better way of breaking down rum style, which is by classifying it according to the island or region that originated the style: Jamaican (pot-still heavy rum), Barbados (a blend of column and pot), Cuban/Spanish (column-still), French (made from cane juice rather than molasses) and so on.

Obviously there are producers that don't sit geographically in any of these regions, but it's likely that the rum they make has taken a lead from one of these styles. This is a system that works alright, but it requires that the drinker has some knowledge of the traditional practices of each region. It also assumes that the rum in question adheres to the expected style of its region. But this often isn't the case. Take Dominica for example, the island's only remaining rum distillery makes rum according to the French standard and yet it is a former British colony. And what about the US, with its hundreds of craft distilleries that produce a whole range of styles. Finally, and perhaps worst of all, it shoves a great number of proudly independent Caribbean and Central American nations under the title of their (generally) former colonial administrator, which is more than a little disrespectful, in my view!

I am of course not the first to recognize this need for new classification, and quite recently there have been great steps towards establishing a global standard for rum categorization. The aim of a new system is simple: build a framework of rum classification that clearly informs the consumer how the product has been made and what it is likely to taste like. With the information clear on every bottle (or from the mouth of every bartender), the consumer will then have everything they need to place a value on the product.

One such system has been developed by two of the biggest names in the rum industry: Luca Gargano of the Italian rum bottler Velier, and Richard Seale of Foursquare distillery in Barbados. Their system goes something like this:

Single Pot-Still Rum – A pot-still rum that is the product of a single distillery;

Single Column-Still Rum – A single column-still rum that is the product of a single distillery;

Single Blended Rum – A blend of pot- and column-still rum that are both the products of a single distillery;

Blended Rum – A rum containing pot-still rum that is the product of more than one distillery;

Rum – A multi-column distilled rum that contains no pot-still rum.

This is a classification system that places a great deal of emphasis on the distillation process and whether the rum is a product of a single distillery or not, and follows closely to the Scotch whisky model. The main intention is to highlight the different approaches to making rum these days: in a traditional distillery (with a pot-still) and in a modern ethanol plant (with multi-column stills). This is important information for consumers, because it highlights the value of rums that are produced in the more traditional, more costly, manner. On the other hand, it fails to effectively communicate flavour. There is no mention of base material, country of origin, maturation or fermentation.

I have devised my own classification system, that is built upon the above system and the system detailed in Martin Cate's excellent *Smuggler's Cove* cocktail book. This system is not as exacting as Seale and Gargano's in its treatment of rums that are the product of a single distillery vs. rums blended from various sources. It also makes no distinction between single-column (Coffey) distillation and multi-column distillation. While I recognize that the two methods can and do make different styles of rum, I also believe that a good system also needs to be a simple system.

Rums can be categorized based on three key criteria:
• How long (if at all) the rum has been aged;
• What base material the rum is made from;
• How the rum has been distilled and/or blended.

The first of these is the age of the rum. Classifying rum by the time it has spent in barrels is quite often misleading. This is because not all producers adhere to the EU and US rules of stating the age of the youngest rum in the bottle, and regulating this is a difficult if not impossible task to undertake. There are also rums that are matured for only a few years, but thanks to the addition of sugar, colourings and other flavourings (see pages 71–74), simulate the characteristics of an older rum. I have debated these practices in other sections of the book, but for the sake of classifying flavour, we are forced to lump them in with rums that are genuinely old, as they taste pretty damn similar. With that in mind, we will be using four different descriptors to communicate maturation: **un-aged**; **aged white**; **aged**; and **extra-aged**.

The second section of the classification concerns the raw material that the rum is made from. Rums made from cane juice (also known as *agricole*) have a different spectrum of flavour and aroma from those made from molasses or cane syrup (cane honey). Here, we will single out rums that are produced from the fermentation of cane juice, by placing "Cane Juice" at the start of the rum's category identifier. I think that it's very difficult to distinguish between

cane syrup and molasses as a base material in a finished product, and a category system with "molasses" or "syrup" in front of every title is too clunky. So these two will be lumped in together and identified by the fact that they do not stipulate "Cane Juice" as their base material.

Distillation is the hardest of the three classification components to communicate, partly because of the diverse range of rum production techniques out there and the blending that follows. But also because these pieces of machinery don't communicate flavour effectively for the average consumer. Too much detail and the system becomes baffling and ineffective, but too little detail and major deviations may get missed and there will be too little information to form an accurate assessment of the product.

This system will make three separate distinctions for distillation: **column-still** (but rather than explicitly state that a rum is made in a column-still, we will simply refer to these spirits as "rum"); **pot-still**; and **blended** (being a blend of pot and column-still rums). The most important distinction here is the pot still, which produces a very different type of liquid when compared to the column. Naturally, a blend of both will offer something, somewhere in-between.

LEFT The world of rum is often a confusing and even misleading place to explore. By building a framework of classification, it will be a much easier and more enjoyable journey.

In practice, our system now offers a complete solution for describing any of the thousands of rums that are out there, produced by hundreds of distilleries, across dozens of unique territories. Whether it's an "Extra-Aged Rum" from Nicaragua, an "Aged-White Blended Rum" from St Lucia, an "Aged Pot-Still Rum" from Jamaica, or an "Un-aged Cane Juice Rum" from Martinique.

BLACK RUM/NAVY STRENGTH/OVERPROOF

Here are three additional classifications of British origin that, although capable of fitting into the above system, are better singled out, as they are more heavily stylized by their strength or the liberal use of colourings than they are by base product, distillation or maturation.

Black Rum is a style of lightly aged or un-aged rum that has been heavily coloured to simulate what might have once been a long-in-barrel style consumed aboard ships. They are typically coloured with caramel or molasses to recreate the effect. This produces a unique rum format, that is both hot and light, yet appearing dense and rich. It's very important to draw a distinction between these rums and extra-aged examples that may have a similar hue, but taste rather different. Some good examples of this style are Gosling's Black Seal, Captain Morgan Original, and Lamb's. The point is, they are still young rums, but their darker appearance has a peculiar effect on our sense of flavour perception, being simultaneously "old"-tasting and light.

Navy Strength is an extension of the Black Rum style, and refers to rums that have been coloured and that are stronger than 50% ABV. Traditionally these rums would have been at least 57% ABV, which is equivalent to the imperial measurement of 100% proof (see page 29). Some examples of Navy Strength rums are: Wood's, Rum XP, Pusser's Overproof and Gosling's 151.

Overproof is a term that can also be used to describe Navy Strength rum, but I tend to use Overproof when referring to un-aged or very lightly aged spirits that are bottled above 50% ABV. Some good examples of this style are: Wray & Nephew White, Sunset Very Strong Rum, and Clarke's Court Pure White Rum.

AGRICOLE AND AOC

For all my moaning about a lack of overriding legislation when it comes to rum-making, this is not the case as far as *rhum agricole* is concerned. This style of rum is known to few people and enjoyed by even fewer, but it is one of the most exciting areas of the rum category and one that is carefully defined by law.

Under EU law, *rhum agricole* must be produced from the freshly pressed juice of sugarcane and must be made in one of nine listed territories including the likes of Guadeloupe, Grenada, Madeira and Réunion. In addition to this, the island of Martinique has an Appellation d'Origine Contrôlée (AOC), which is similar to the EU's Protected Designation of Origin, that sets out rules concerning production practices, distillation equipment, and even cane-harvesting periods for any product wishing to class itself as AOC Martinique Rhum Agricole (see below).

The only problem with the EU's *rhum agricole* definition is that it doesn't capture all rums made from sugarcane juice as a base material, which can leave some rums locked in a state of limbo if they don't comply with certain aspects of the edict. To make matters more confusing, the term *agricole* was not historically used to describe sugarcane juice-based spirits, but to signify a plantation-based distillery versus a larger urban distillery regardless of the material used. The plantation distillery with its immediate source of sugar was *agricole* (agricultural) and the large urban distillery receiving molasses was *industriel* ("industrial").

For me, any rum produced using fresh cane juice as the base material and where the use of cane juice is perceivable in the final product (I'm looking at you, Barbancourt distillery can reasonably be called a *rhum agricole* according to the modern definition – regardless of where it actually comes from. To make a rum from cane juice, it's essential that the cane grows nearby, and that physical link to the land – irrespective of distillery size – is what really exemplifies the style.

AOC MARTINIQUE RHUM AGRICOLE

This classification is by far the most rigorous among any legal classification of rum. It starts with the plantation itself, which must be on the island of Martinique and must fall within one of 23 designated municipalities that lie mostly in the centre of the island. Cultivation yields are limited to 120 tons (132 US tons) of sugarcane per hectare, which is designed to limit the amount of fertilizer used and to keep agricultural practices sustainable. Harvest must take place between January 1 and August 31 every year, and only certain chemicals are permitted to be used.

The wort used for fermentation must be composed only of the juice of the plant (and water) and must be a minimum of 14° Brix and a pH of at least 4.7 – both of these measures are there to promote the harvesting of fully ripe cane, but they also limit fermentation problems due to insufficient sugars. Distillation takes place in a column still comprising 5–9

ABOVE Just your average Martinican supermarket, where a litre of AOC Martinique *rhum agricole* costs a mere €4.95 (£4.20 or $5).

rectifying plates and at least 15 copper or stainless steel stripping plates. The spirit must come off the still at an average of 65–75% ABV. These measures are aimed at limiting undesirable heavy alcohols in the final product.

The legislation also stretches to label, where *blanc* must be rested in steel for at least 3 months; *élevé sous bois* must be aged for at least 12 months and contain at least 20 g (0.7 oz) of congeners (flavour-giving compounds) per 100 litres (26.5 US gallons) of pure alcohol; and *vieux* must be aged for at least 3 years in casks no larger than 650 litres (172 US gallons) and contain at least 325 g (11.5 oz) congeners per 100 litres (26.5 US gallons) of pure alcohol.

BLENDERS AND BOTTLERS

Without the blenders of this world, it's quite likely that all of us would all still be driving along worn distillery paths, returning with a jerry can full of white rum hanging from each arm. From the 19th century onwards, the blenders formed the missing link between wholesale product and marketable brand, transforming rum from industrial oddity to trustworthy liquor. The famed rum distilleries of the New World would never have evolved into what they are today were it not for the hard graft of the blenders.

Many distilleries conduct some sort of in-house blending (different ages of rum, or different distillation marques), but the rums in this section are concerned with blended spirits from multiple distilleries and multiple countries of origin. Rum has always been an international spirit, and blending is a celebration of that. Blended rums are some of the oldest-surviving and best-selling spirit brands in the world. A good blend is a mark of dependence; a familiar friend in a sea of obscurity.

Also deserving of our attentions are the independent bottlers. On the face of it, it's strange that a distillery wouldn't wish to bottle rum under their own label. But some operations specialize in selling rum to third parties, and others are just happy to sell rum by any means possible – be it by the bottle, barrel or shipping container. In some instances, a distillery might have gone silent (closed down) in which case there is nobody or no brand to bottle the product. But where there are casks left lying around, it stands to reason that somebody will be happy to pay for them. Independent bottling of rum is not as commonplace yet as it is with whisky, but there is a growing market for it. And as we shall

see in the pages that follow, some of the best rums on the planet are sold this way.

BANKS

Banks is named after Sir Joseph Banks, the explorer and botanist who sailed alongside Captain Cook, and who backed a certain William Bligh as the governor of New South Wales – an appointment that ultimately led to the Rum Rebellion of 1808. Banks wasn't a rum blender, or distiller, but it's certain that he would have enjoyed a tot or two during his time at sea.

The brand was founded in 2010 by Arnaud de Trabuc and R. John Pellaton, and is blended by E&A Scheer (see pages 81–82) in Amsterdam. Trabuc and Pellaton have certainly got their money's worth out of the Dutch blending powerhouse: the core expression contains spirit from Jamaica, Trinidad, Guyana and Barbados, as well as Batavia Arrack from Java – a type of Indonesian cane spirit that is traditionally used in the punches of old.

Taking liquids from such a broad range of sources could quite easily result in a complete mess, but this is top-drawer sipping spirit, and a liquid that flags up all sorts of opportunities as a mixing spirit. Don't be fooled by the numbers on the bottle: these are not age statements but a reference to the number of islands and territories that feature in the bottle. In Banks 5, there are chewy pot-still esters, just as there are vegetal agricole notes. Banks 7 ups the ante even further, with the addition of rums sourced from Panama and Guatemala. The Central American influence cuts through some of that youthful bad temper and carries with it a range of confected qualities.

CAPTAIN MORGAN

The Captain Morgan brand was launched by Seagram's in 1944 and now sells over 10 million 9-litre (2.4-US gallon) cases of rum a year, which makes it the second biggest international rum brand after Bacardí. The story of this brand is an interesting one, in respect of the big business approach to production, as well as the tale of Sir Henry Morgan himself, who was once a real person. Every bottle of Captain Morgan has a grinning illustration of the "The Captain" on the label, but few people are aware that the real life "Captain" was one of the most ruthless and unprincipled villains of his age, with a lifetime of deeds far darker than the colour of his namesake rum.

Morgan was born in south Wales in 1635, the son of a relatively wealthy farmer. He had no inclination to follow in his father's muddy footsteps however, so instead followed the lead of his uncles, who were both distinguished military men. Some accounts suggest that Morgan was captured and shipped off to the Caribbean as a white indentured servant, which was arguably an even worse existence than that of the black African slave, who were considered more valuable. Other accounts state that he willingly joined the Royal Navy as a junior officer. Either way, that's where he ended up, and at the age of 19, he found himself in the Caribbean fighting alongside Admiral Penn when the English captured Jamaica from the Spanish in 1655.

Morgan settled in Jamaica for around five years, during which time he became hardened by the cruelty of existence in the nascent colony. At some point Morgan was recruited by a pirate crew, which turned out to be a profession that he was rather good at. After a few years, Morgan and a few of his new associates pooled their resources and bought a ship, and Morgan was nominated as Captain.

Pirating was a little like the Mafia in those days, and the head of the organization was the Dutchman Edward Mansvelt. He controlled hundreds of pirate ships, and made Morgan the "vice-admiral" of his fleet. These two plundered many Spanish colonies in the years that followed, setting up island bases off the South American coast, but always returning to Jamaica to divide up the booty.

As Morgan's success and notoriety grew, so too did the size of the fleet he commanded, which at times totalled up to 37 ships. As grand as that may sound, the brutality of encounters with the Captain garnered him a reputation as one of the most barbarous individuals of

S^r HEN MORGAN

RIGHT Henry Morgan was made a baronet in 1674 by King Charles II – quite a change in the pirate's fortunes considering that the King had ordered his arrest two years earlier.

80 HOW RUM IS MADE

the time. During sieges, he used nuns and priests as human shields, correctly predicting that the Spanish would be too pious to fire arrows at holy men and women. After successfully taking the fort town of Portobello on Panama's coast, Morgan personally knocked on doors, forcing the town's residents to provide information that would lead to the discovery of hidden gold caches. Those who resisted were tortured in various cruel and creative ways: men were strung up by their testicles while their wives were raped. Others had burning twigs tied between their fingers, or were stretched by their thumbs and toes until something gave way.

Morgan's most legendary feat occurred in 1671, during the sacking of Panama. At that time, Panama was the second-largest city in the new world, and a key New Spain trading route for Spanish conquistadors, as well as being home to a thriving mercantile community. Morgan knew this, and in January of that year landed at San Lorenzo with an "army" of 1,200 men. They marched overland to Panama City, and despite the larger numbers and fortifications of the Spanish defenders, they were terrified of Morgan and abandoned their defences. The city burned for four straight weeks.

The sacking of Panama stands today as one of the most extraordinary military campaigns ever fought.

After Panama, Henry Morgan returned to a Jamaica much changed from the one he had left. In the Treaty of Madrid, signed in 1670, England had agreed to suppress piracy in return for Spanish recognition of its sovereignty in Jamaica. In 1672, Morgan was transported back to England to be tried for piracy, but he was received more as a romantic hero than as a vicious criminal.

Relations with Spain deteriorated once again, and in 1674, he was made a baronet. Later that year, he returned to Jamaica as Lieutenant Governor Sir Henry Morgan, even serving as acting governor from 1680 to 1682. He died in 1688 – rich, respectable, morbidly obese and an enduring contradiction to the adage that crime does not pay.

You might be wondering by this point why anybody would feel compelled to base a rum brand around this man. But it has to be said that Morgan's crooked past has done little to damage the success of the brand. In the eyes of many people, high-strength alcohol has always walked a fine line between social lubricant and moral contaminant. Perhaps "the Captain" represents that better than most. Still, it's quite amusing that Diageo, which has been the brand owner since 2001, currently use the tagline "Live like the Captain" to promote the brand. But I suppose it's an improvement over the altogether more sinister-sounding "Everybody's Got a Little Captain in Them!", which was retired in 2014.

The production specifics of Captain Morgan are vague to say the least. Jamaica's Clarendon distillery produces a lot of rum for the international version of the blend, and Diageo's Virgin Island operation does the same for the US version. It's possible that the story ends there, but there are rumours that wholesale rum shipments occasionally arrive at these distilleries too, so who's to say that Diageo aren't blending in other rums?

E&A SCHEER

If you fancy yourself as a bit of a rum blender, you're going to need more than just a finely-tuned palate and a love of cane spirits to build a brand. A good list of distillery contacts, warehouse space, logistical expertise and some skills in commercial negotiation are all essential. Not to mention bottling and packaging equipment and storage for all this stuff. You cannot simply walk up to the door of a few Caribbean distilleries and expect to walk out with your own blended bottle. And that's just what you need to get you started. What about when certain rums run out? How do you go about adapting the blend?

The long and short of this is that you can't do it on your own, and the truth is that very few blenders do. Help is at hand however, in the form of the Amsterdam-based rum broker and blender E&A Scheer.

Even though you'll struggle to find their name on any bottle of rum, this blending powerhouse is still worth a mention. They are one of the most important gears in the global rum engine and for the superstitious readers among you, this is the rum world's "man behind the curtain". Indeed, E&A Scheer would prefer to remain unknown, as their business is in the supply and building of other people's brands, not their own. And they supply a lot of brands. Exactly how many is a bit of a mystery, but I think it's fair to assume that the majority of the blended rums out there pass through the doors of E&A Scheer.

In fact, some would say that this company is so deeply entrenched in the rum category, that establishing a blended rum brand of any worth without their assistance would likely prove a cripplingly difficult endeavour – if not impossible.

The "E" and "A" of the company name are the initials of Evert and Anthonie Scheer, Dutch brothers who formed a trading company in the Amsterdam in the middle of the 18th century. Originally intended as a general purpose trading company, by the 19th century, the company had sensibly narrowed its focus to the trading and blending of rums and Batavia Arrack (an Indonesian cane-based spirit). They were doing well enough at that to propel their company forward in the rum business for the next 250 years.

These days, E&A Scheer employ 18 people from their Amsterdam-based offices, and buy rum from 20 different countries. As individual batches of rum arrive in Amsterdam, they're nosed and blended down into a couple of dozen "intermediate" blends and stored in neutral containers so that no further maturation can occur. These blends are described with names known only to the blenders and form the building blocks of the multitude of finished products that E&A Scheer produce. From 200 litres (53 US gallons) to 25,000 litres (6,600 US gallons), E&A Scheer will tailor your blend to your specific tastes, budget and regional preferences.

E&A Scheer also owns the Main Rum Company, located in Liverpool in the UK. The Amsterdam office focuses on younger rums and blending; the Main Rum Company focuses on older, vintage rums, some of which are still in cask and therefore still maturing.

ELEMENTS EIGHT

Elements Eight is a British independent rum blender who source all of their liquids from the St. Lucia Distillers Ltd. The brand was launched in 2006 by Carl Stephenson and Andreas Redlefsen, who both previously worked for J. Wray & Nephew. They partnered with the late Lauri Barnard of St. Lucia Distillers to produce a blend that celebrates eight suggested factors of rum flavour influence: terroir, cane, fermentation,

GOSLINGS

Bermuda is not the kind of island that gets stumbled upon by accident. That is, unless you happen to be the Spanish navigator Juan de Bermúdez, who was probably the first human to ever lay eyes on the archipelago, in 1503. This cluster of islands has a total area of just 53.5 square kilometres (21 square miles), but is over 1,000 km (620 miles) from the nearest sensible-sized chunk of land on the east coast of North Carolina. It's also around 1,500 km (930 miles) north of the Caribbean, placing it well above the Tropic of Cancer where it enjoys warm summers and mild winters on account of the warm Gulf Stream currents that emanate from the Caribbean. There's little in the way of arable land on Bermuda, so when coupled with its mild climate, it's altogether a pretty poor place for growing sugarcane. And it's for that reason there's absolutely no history of rum distillation on the island.

Indeed, were it not for William and James Gosling, it's likely that Bermuda would be known only for its long surf-shorts and mysterious triangle. The year was 1806, when the father and son duo set sail from Gravesend in Kent, England. They spent three desperate months attempting to cross the Atlantic, on a voyage bound for Virginia carrying a cargo of wine and spirits worth £10,000 (£1.2 million or $1.5 million today). Tired, dejected and probably quite wet (though not without a stiff drink to raise the spirits), they headed for the nearest port, which was St George's in Bermuda. Any port in a storm, so the saying goes, but St George's must have appeared an especially

distillation, ageing, blending, filtration and water.

The product has a noticeably dry characteristic, which made it great for mixing with, and by 2008 it had become the go-to premium speed-rail rum for many of the top London bars. Just like Pyrat (see pages 92–93), here was a rum to challenge the clichéd convention of Caribbean rum, through preaching about process and provenance. The product was also packaged in an unusual, box-shaped bottle. Ten years on, and it feels as though Elements Eight has lost some of that initial momentum. The packaging has been refreshed, and while the glassware is a little more sensible than the previous long, boxy bottle, the labelling still leaves a little to be desired in this author's opinion. The liquid on the other hand gives little cause for complaint. That's not surprising given the provenance of the juice, but this is carefully balanced stuff that succeeds at highlighting the various elements of rum-making.

numerous, many spirit- and liqueur-makers opted to recycle the bottles as packaging for their own premium range of liquids. Getting a supply of empty Champagne bottles was quite easy for the Goslings, thanks to the many officers in the nearby Royal Navy Dockyards, who had a healthy appetite for good French wine.

In the 1860s, the business passed into the hands of Ambrose Gosling's three sons, William, Edmund and Charles, and the name of the company changed to Gosling Brothers. The family marketed their first rum, which was known simply as "Old Rum". Over 150 years later, Old Rum is still available in dark Champagne-style bottles with a thick black wax seal on top.

That wax has a lot to answer for, as it's thanks to that gloopy black seal, which speaks of tarred decks and greased chains, that Gosling Brothers rum was soon referred to as the "Black Seal" rum. It became the most popular brand on the island, to the point where it was said that to be a true Bermudian, a man needed only to do three things: "attend Trinity Church, read the Royal Gazette and buy his rum at Goslings." In the 1960s, the Black Seal became officially part of their branding, when their labels changed to include an image of a black seal juggling a barrel of rum.

It's certain that the constant presence of the Bermuda Garrison (which existed primarily to defend Bermuda's Royal Navy Dockyard) contributed to the success of the rum brand. Military personnel, and particularly those at sea, are known to enjoy a tot of rum, and Goslings served as a taste of the island to servicemen both on the island and back

favourable place, because they scrapped all plans of completing their charter, bought a shop, and William invited his second son, Ambrose, to the island to help them out.

James and Ambrose's grocer's shop was originally on the King's Parade in the island's capital, Hamilton. They traded in all kinds of goods, from textiles to coffee, rice, sugar and of course, rum. As was common for the time, a grocer would produce a proprietary blend of rum, brandy or sherry, from stocks that arrived through the port. The locals would turn up to the store with an empty container and fill it straight from the barrel. Few spirits (and least of all rum) were bottled in glass in the 19th century, since it was too costly to manufacture and ship the bottles. Champagne was one drink for which glass bottling was a pre-requisite, however (due to the requirement of fizz) and as these bottles became more in Britain. The Navy even erected a ginger beer bottling plant on the island so that they had something to mix the rum with.

Gosling Brothers Ltd. is still a family enterprise, currently run by the seventh generation of the Gosling family: Malcolm Gosling Jr., (the great-great-great-grandson of Ambrose Gosling); his sister, Nancy Gosling, who is the CEO; and his cousin, the Right Worshipful Charles Gosling, who is the current mayor of Hamilton.

Goslings Black Seal is a blend of rums from Trinidad, Guyana, Barbados and Jamaica. The distillate arrives at 9 Dundonald St. in Hamilton in stainless-steel tanks, where it is aged and blended according to an old family recipe that quite likely calls for a large measure of caramel colouring to give the rum that rich, inky appearance. The portion destined for the local market stays behind. The rest goes back in the tanks and journeys by sea to Port Elizabeth, New Jersey, and thence by rail to Bardstown, Kentucky, where it is diluted, bottled and cased for shipment around the world.

JOHN WATLING'S

While it is widely acknowledged that Columbus's favoured island – or the one he believed most likely to contain gold – was Hispaniola, the first terra firma the navigator sighted after 29 days at sea was in fact the Bahamas. The present day archipelago is made up of over 700 individual islands and islets, so as to which one specifically Columbus landed on October 12 1492 is a matter of great debate (though it seems generally accepted that it was the island of San Salvador). Once on shore, he encountered the Lucayan people, a branch of the Arawakan-speaking Taínos,

and true to form he enslaved the "sweet and gentle" people, swiftly transporting his cargo onward, to Cuba and Hispaniola.

For over a century, the islands were ignored by the Spanish who deemed them too small to be of any use, and they remained uninhabited until the mid-1600s. But their secluded position and close proximity to wealthy colonies like Sainte-Domingue and Santo Domingo, soon made the Bahamas an ideal hideout for buccaneers and pirates. Meanwhile, a newly established British colony of Charles Town on the island of New Providence, became the target of Spanish corsair raids, culminating in its complete destruction by fire in 1684. It was rebuilt, and given a new name: Nassau.

Nassau didn't fare much better than its predecessor, however, suffering sustained attacks from the combined Franco-Spanish fleet between 1703 and 1706. With the city all-but deserted, pirates quickly took

BELOW Authentic packaging, decent liquid and a nice backstory. This rum will do well.

up occupancy. And so it was that the "Republic of Pirates" was formed, which, at the height of its power had over 1,000 pirate members, all living in a quasi-democracy under the jurisdiction of their magistrate, Edward Teach (aka Blackbeard). Besides Blackbeard, the "Republic" was dominated by two more famous pirates who were bitter rivals: Benjamin Hornigold and Henry Jennings. Hornigold was Teach's mentor, along with "Black" Sam Bellamy and Stede Bonnet. Jennings was mentor to Charles Vane, "Calico" Jack Rackham, Anne Bonny and Mary Read.

Nassau was the Port Royal for the next generation of pirates, but unlike the Jamaican town, this place was entirely operated by criminals, former sailors, indentured servants and runaway slaves. These were tumultuous times in the Caribbean, but among all the anarchy, Nassau offered freedom for everyone; men and women of colour could be equal citizens, and leaders were chosen or deposed by a vote.

But as their numbers swelled, establishing a fighting force strong enough to take on Royal Navy frigates, the situation as far as the Navy was concerned had become too unstable. In 1718, just five years after the establishment of the Republic, the Navy conducted a strategic eradication of all the pirates in the region, and as many as 600 pirates were killed or captured by British forces in that year. The assault was so efficient that on some occasions up to eight men "swang off" the same post in Nassau. The recapture of Nassau marked the beginning of the end of the Golden Era of Piracy.

Back to the modern era, and Bacardí opened a distillery here in 1965, but it closed in 2009, leaving a big rum-shaped hole on the islands. Now that's a big hole to fill, but in 2013 it was – to some extent at least – plugged, by the John Watling's distillery, located in the historic Buena Vista Estate in Downtown Nassau.

The use of the word "distillery" is a touch misleading in this case because it is in fact not a distillery at all, but a blending house. John Watling's is named after one of the Bahamas' most notorious privateers of the 17th century. John (or sometimes George) Watling served under Captain Bartholomew Sharp, plundering the east coast of Central America, unsettling Spanish colonial interests through systematic raids along Panama and Honduras and befriending Mosquito Indians (who take their name from the word *miskito*, a reference to their mixed Indian and African blood) even to the point of taking one, who he named "Will", under his wing in a Lone Ranger/Tonto sort of scenario.

Watling and Sharp took down dozens of Spanish ships in their time, amassing a small fortune. When the crew mutinied against Sharp, Watling became the new leader, known by many as the "Pious Pirate" since he observed the Sabbath and forbade gambling. Later on, Watling established his headquarters on San Salvador in the Bahamas, where it was

ABOVE Bottling at Watling – big or small, fast or slow, I always find bottling lines mesmerizing.

rumoured that he buried a considerable cache of treasure.

Thanks to his famed escapades in the area, the island was nicknamed John Watling's after him. And now, more recently, Watling has a distillery to add to that.

LAMB'S

Rum blenders plied their trade at an early age in the 19th century. In 1849, Alfred Lamb was just 22-years-old when he set up as a wine merchant and spirits blender. He did have a leg up in to the business, mind you, thanks to his father, William Lamb, who was a respected wine and spirit importer in London. It would be rum with which the Lamb name would become eternally synonymous, though, and Alfred allegedly used a mixed bag of rums from 18 different Caribbean territories, including Barbados, Guyana, Jamaica and Trinidad, to formulate his first Navy blend.

The story continues that Lamb used to store his rums in vaults that sat beneath the River Thames. The cool, cellar environment wasn't subject to seasonal fluctuations in temperature or large fluctuations from day to night, and this is reckoned to be one of the secrets behind the unexpectedly smooth taste of his rum. The only problem with the tale is that Lamb's offices were on Great Tower Street, which is located at least 100 metres (330 ft) from the banks of the Thames and thus was unlikely to have cellars stretching so far.

Alfred was joined by his son, Charles H. Lamb, in 1875 when Charles was just 16, and the company later became known as Alfred Lamb & Sons. Charles blended rum right through his father's death, in 1895, and right up until he retired in the 1920s. On May 11 1941, Alfred Lamb & Son were bombed out of

ABOVE Above all else, blending requires an understanding of how barrels work and how best to utilize them.

their London premises on Great Tower Street during the Blitz. On the same evening, another rum merchants, E. H. Keeling & Son, who were famous for bottling "Old Demerara Rum", also lost their premises to an air strike. Portal, Dingwall & Norris (yet another rum merchant) took pity on both Lamb and Keeling and allowed them to share their premises at 40 Eastcheap, which was just a block up the road. Five years later, the three companies merged to form United Rum Merchants.

The brand was tossed about during various mergers and acquisitions during the 1980s, and finally ended up in the hands of Corby Spirits in Canada, who still own it today and license the brand to Pernod Ricard UK. Canada and the UK also happen to be the brand's two biggest markets, where it has more or less established itself as the de facto Navy Rum offering. In the UK especially, there's hardly a pub that doesn't have a dusty hexagonal bottle of Lamb's permanently stuck to a back bar shelf. Lamb's continued to bottle some of their rum at true Navy Strength (57%) right up until the 1970s, and decanters of these have become highly collectable. If you hunt around internet auction sites, you might also encounter 100% Demerara examples too.

The standard "Genuine Navy Rum" blend is today bottled at 40% ABV and still comprises rums from various Caribbean islands. All of the rums used are matured for a minimum of one year, which comes as quite a shock, given the dark colour of the liquid. But like so many of its seafaring brethren, Lamb's brazenly practises the time-honoured tradition of blackening overproof rum into something that looks as though it has been stashed in a oak barrel since before the Navy rum ration was abolished.

If you've a desire for a sweeter style of Lamb in your life, the core expression has more recently been joined by "Lamb's Spiced" (not to be confused with Spiced Lamb – a dish on an Indian restaurant menu) and "Lamb's Spiced Cherry Rum". I wouldn't bother with either.

LEMON HART

Lemon Hart was a Cornish-born man (just like yours truly) of Jewish descent. In 1720, Hart's grandfather, Abraham, arrived in the town of Penzance – a market town with a harbour, and the most westerly town in England. Abraham established himself there as a goldsmith. Things went well for the family, who over the next 50 years, diversified their interests into shipping and the importation of Jamaican rum, becoming one of the most successful family-run businesses in the region. The business passed on to the next generation in the form of Lazarus Hart (Abraham's son) who, through a combination of bad luck and stupidity, managed to sink an expensive ship and rile up the local Customs house, to the

BELOW Looks like a nice day for drinking rum on the beach in a bright yellow suit, wouldn't you say?

Have a GOOD RUM for your money

point where he was forced to sell the business. Fortunately, things picked back up again, and when he finally died in 1803, he left the floundering business to his only son, Lemon.

A strange name, perhaps, although "Lemon" is a historic surname in Cornwall. When life gave him lemons, Lemon chose to make money, developing a sideline of ship brokering and ownership in Penzance and accelerating the wine and spirit trade right up to the next level.

The "Lemon Hart" trading company was established in 1804, and in the same year, he began bottling rum under that name too. It wasn't too long before Hart's growing empire became the official supplier of rum to the Royal Navy, and by the time Lemon died in 1845, the company had relocated to the Isle of

Dogs in London and were supplying the Royal Navy with 455,000 litres (120,000 US gallons) of rum annually – equivalent to nearly 10% of Jamaica's total export volume for that year.

The brand became incredibly popular in the 1950s, partly thanks to a viral advertising campaign that was illustrated by Ronald Searle. The adverts depicted a slender gentleman dressed in a lemon-coloured suit, knocking back rum in various implausible situations. The tagline was "Have a Good Rum for your Money".

These day's Lemon Hart is available in three expressions: Original 1804, Blackpool Spiced Rum, and Lemon Hart 151. All of them are made and mixed at the Diamond Distillery in Guyana. The most famous of the three is the 151, which has for a long time been a popular overproof go-to for Tiki enthusiasts.

MATUSALEM

Matusalem enjoyed some success in the early 21st century, at around the time that I first started tending bar. Playing off its Cuban roots, it was seen as a valid challenger to Bacardí in a similar way as Havana Club was. It turned out that the brand had more in common with the former, however, as Matusalem is yet another Cuban rum dynasty that fled the island during Castro's Revolution. Indeed, Matusalem was founded in Santiago de Cuba by the Camps Hermanos (the Camps brothers) just 10 years after Bacardí, in 1872. The trio of brothers had some experience working with sherry and Cognac back in Spain, and they applied the principles of solera ageing to their Ron Matusalem Extra Viejo. The name "Matusalem" is the Spanish word for "Methuselah", the Old Testament patriarch who was said to have lived for more than 900 years.

By the middle of the 20th century,

Matusalem was in fierce competition with Bacardí, and the two brands regularly employed aggressive sales tactics to undercut one another. Matusalem would have been far better off spending their time establishing overseas operations (like Bacardí) which might have saved them from becoming the revolutionary collateral damage that they did.

These days the product is still made in Santiago, only this Santiago is in the Dominican Republic. The brand are not overly forthcoming when it comes to details; certainly they don't own a distillery in the Dominican Republic, and it seems questionable that they are filling their own casks, so it's for that reason that I have categorized them as a blender.

MEZAN

Mezan touts itself as "the untouched rum" – that is to say, it has had absolutely no sugar or colouring added to it. As such, some members of the range are surprisingly straw-coloured in their appearance, which just goes to show the quantity of caramel that gets added to many of the world's favourite rums. For me, this is a very refreshing approach to rum marketing, and a welcome antidote to heavily doctored liquids emerging from some producers. My only regret is that the rums in the Mezan range are cut to 40% ABV prior to bottling, it feels like a lost opportunity to raise the bar a little and package at a higher strength. Currently there are four rums in the range: two Jamaican, one of which is a blend and the other sourced from an early Worthy Park distillate from 2005; a bottling of a 1996 Caroni from Trinidad; and a Panama bottling from 2006.

PLANTATION

If you want to see one of the most diverse rum cellars in the world, you're

BELOW The great thing about Plantation is that it's almost possible to explore the entire breadth of the rum category without straying from their impressive array of expressions.

better off in France than the Caribbean. Nobody knows wood like the French, and in Cognac they have been nurturing the relationship between oak and spirit for some 400 years through their use of fine French oak, but also in the arcane practice of élevage (see page 69). Sadly, Cognac is a spirit category that has struggled to evolve with the times, and its outdated marketing and bureaucracy have made for a rather standardized range of products in the market. One man set on changing this is Alexandre Gabriel, frontman of Maison Ferrand, one of the most progressive Cognac houses in the region. Ferrand are not only interested in innovating grape spirits, Alexandre has also spent the last 20 years nurturing a growing rum business that goes by the name of Plantation.

Alexandre bought the struggling Maison Ferrand Cognac house in 1989, when he was just 23. He built the business by travelling from bar to bar, sleeping on sofas, and simultaneously training for 10 years as a cellar master. While the business was still in its infancy,

he sold some Cognac to a Jamaican distillery who later defaulted on payment. In return – and in keeping with trade arrangements from a few centuries ago – Alexandre accepted payment in rum. This was to be the catalyst for Alexandre's fascination with the rum category and the establishment of his rum business, starting with the launch, in France, of the Kaniché brand.

Alexandre didn't want to just source and bottle rum, however – he wanted to place his own mark on the spirit, a signature that would amplify the base characteristics of the liquid and celebrate the distillery and the island in which it was born. So, using a bit of that Cognac know-how he began conducting additional 1–3 year maturation cycles in Cognac casks on all the rums he bought.

Kaniché found some success (and it is still available today as a 100% Barbadian blend), but Alexandre's curiosity was piqued, as he discovered new rums from islands and distilleries that had previously been under the radar. By the early 2000s, Plantation had released dozens of expressions from as many countries, and established themselves across Europe as one of rum's greatest independent bottlers.

In accordance with the practices of Champagne production, Plantation add a dosage to their rum, which is another way of saying "they sweeten it". But this isn't just any old sugar. It's a blend of white rum and sugar syrup that has been aged in Cognac casks for 10–12 years. More than a sweetener, Plantation's dosage is a delicious fingerprint that's smeared all over the contents of every single expression they produce. Disciples of the anti-sugaring campaign (see pages 71–73) have criticized Plantation in the past for its sugaring policy, but the fact that the brand is transparent about sweetening, and that the sweetening itself is in keeping with the traditional wine- and Cognac-making practices of France, as well as the fact that the rums taste excellent... well, that makes it difficult to contest.

Plantation have 14 expressions in their core range, which includes three expressions geared towards mixed drinks: 3-Stars, a white mixing rum; Original Dark, a black rum; and Plantation Overproof, an aged overproof rum. The "Signature Blends" is a range that's better suited to sipping or light mixing and include Plantation 5-year-old, a benchmark aged blend; 20th Anniversary, a curiously coconut-y blend of 12–20-year-old Barbados rums; and a pair of extra-aged rums. From there, you have a bunch of vintage rums, which are effectively the single malts of the range – each from a specific distillery and produced in a specific year. Lastly, there's the "Single Cask" range, which change annually and feature rums from a dozen different distilleries, finished in ex-wine casks and individually bottled and numbered from – that's right – a single cask.

A tour of Alexandre's warehouses reveals even more experiments that are currently underway. Thanks to a partnership with Mackmyra, the Swedish whisky distillery, Plantation are maturing rums in 50-litre (13-US gallon) ex-whisky casks. Plantation are exploring alternative wood types for their casks too, such as chestnut and acacia. Ever the innovator, Alexandre has plans afoot to place a warehouse on a barge floating on the River Seine, just to see how the gentle rocking of the boat will affect the ongoing maturation process.

PUSSER'S

When the last Navy rum ration was dispensed at "6 bells to the forenoon" (11am) on July 31 1970, it marked the end of 315 years of Royal Navy tradition. The remaining stocks of Navy rum were sold at auction and they quickly spread far and wide among bars and private collections, disappearing like spilled rum through cracks on the deck of a ship. The vast majority of this rum was drunk before the turn of the millennium, but it is still possible to find rare flagons of the stuff floating around auction houses, as well as smaller packagings, like the rather pricey "Black Tot: The Last Consignment" bottling that's sold by Speciality Drinks in the UK – yours for a mere £650 ($800) a bottle.

If your budget doesn't stretch that far, there is an alternative. In 1979, nearly a decade after the Royal Navy abandoned the custom of the daily tot of rum, Charles Tobias, an entrepreneurial sailor-type based in the British Virgin

RIGHT An iconic bottle, with some rope, naturally. Funnily enough, Pusser's 15-year old rum does taste rope-y.

Islands, founded Pusser's Rum after obtaining the rights to the blending information for the naval rum ration along with the licence to use the Royal Navy flag on his packaging. The terms of the deal also stipulated that Pusser's donate a proportion of annual profits to the Royal Navy Sailor's fund (also know as the "Tot Fund"). And they still do. In 2015 alone they handed over £25,000 ($31,000), which will be used for a whole range of projects that support the active and ex-servicemen and women of the Royal Navy.

Back to the rum: the name Pusser's comes from a corruption of the word "purser", which was the former title of the the ship's store man – the man upon whose shoulders it fell to ensure that sufficient quantities of rum were stocked aboard the ship and that it was of suitable quality. And by "quality", I mean strength, and this was determined by conducting a proof test with gunpowder (see page 29).

Pusser's rum is aged rum comprising "predominantly pot-still rum". Guyanese rum certainly features heavily (it contains some spirit from the Port Mourant still at DDL) and so too does rum from the Angostura distillery in Trinidad. Some of the expressions also contain rum from Barbados, too.

The blending and bottling of these rums all takes place on the British Virgin Islands, which also happens to be the home of the Pusser's Pub and the Painkiller cocktail (see pages 126–27).

The bottle strength of this rum has been fiddled with a few times over the years. When Pusser's iconic "blue label" rum was first launched in 1980, it was bottled at the original Navy strength of 54.5% ABV. At one time in Germany, it was even possible to pick up a rare "green label" Pusser's that was bottled at

75% ABV! But in 2012, the brand quietly dropped the alcohol percentage of its "blue label" down to 40% while simultaneously launching Pusser's "Gunpowder Strength", which, in spite of being a fantastic name, is seemingly the same 54.5% "'blue label" rum you would have bought as standard a few years back. Apparently the reason for lowering the alcohol content was so that the brand could supply British Naval bases, which are forbidden from holding spirits that are above 40% ABV. It's probably the best excuse for watering down rum that I've come across.

PYRAT

Whether it's pronounced *pye-rat* or *pi-rat* (nobody is sure) Pyrat is worthy of some recognition as one of the first blenders (along with Plantation) to elevate rum to the realms of "super-premium". But there's a funny thing about the "super-premium" designation – the fact that it's awarded only on the basis of price, not quality. I'm not saying that Pyrat is a terrible rum, but it is certainly divisive. When I first started bartending it, Pyrat's "Pistol" expression was a bit of a cult hero, partly because it was packaged in a lean "pistol" shaped bottle, which was, and still is, atypical to the category's traditional "clothing". Innovative as it perhaps once was, the rum world has moved on, and these days Pyrat is not shown the same degree of affection it once was. Why? Well, the fact that "Pistol" is no longer available, hasn't done it any favours, but the main reason is because of the way it tastes. There really is only one readily available expression of Pyrat available today – XO – and either it's the colour of the label and the orange ribbon working some serious subliminal magic, or these rums have a strangely pervasive tangerine aroma.

ABOVE Orange, inside and out. You can do this yourself with a bottle of Grand Marnier and the rum of your choosing.

The official home of Pyrat is the tiny island Anguila, named for the French word for "eel" on account of its long and slippery shape. The rum was originally blended on the island from a mix of "nine pot-still rums", but these days there's little information about Pyrat's current production process available to the common man. I did some delving and it seems that the Anguila connection is in danger of becoming a rather difficult claim to sustain for the Pyrat brand. In 2010, The Anguila Rum Company, who make Pyrat, were bought by Patrón Spirits, who are based in Nevada and best known for their hugely successful Tequila brand by the same name. Since then, the rum has been blended at the Diamond distillery in Guyana, and made from a blend of high-ester Demerara rum and "other Caribbean rums". Whether these rums are all matured in Guyana too remains a mystery, but they are certainly bottled there – on a private bottling line, no less – which does beg the question, where exactly does Anguila fit into the story today? And while we're in the mood for

questioning things: why is there a cartoon picture of a Buddha on the bottle? This is the sort of information that a brand website might normally provide, but at the time of writing, Pyrat's has been under maintenance for an extended period.

Equally mysterious is the story of this rum, which is about as tenuous a tale as any I have come across. It starts with C.J. Planter, a travelling seaman, who, in the early 1800s, abandoned ship and fell in love with an Anguilan girl. She turned out to be the illegitimate daughter of a local plantation owner and the local witch. Planter moved in with the family, and shortly afterwards, the mill and house burned to the ground, killing the girl's father. Planter took over the running of the estate, and in order to woo his future wife, decided to make her a rum. Enlisting the help of her witch-mother they created the Pyrat rum blend, which soon became the talk of the island because it was rumoured to be imbued with mystical powers.

The name is simply an alternative spelling of the word "pirate", but I could find no historical evidence of a rum ever existing under this name. As for the omnipresent orange aroma, there have been rumours that some of the casks used to mature the spirit were previously used to mature orange liqueurs (such as Grand Marnier), which would certainly explain a lot. In some respects, practising this kind of thing is no different to using a sherry or port cask, but one does have to question when wine or liqueur casks stop being a "seasoning" and start becoming an added flavouring. In the case of Pyrat, I do wonder if the balance is slightly lost, but if you're a fan of orange in your alcohol you need look no further.

SMITH & CROSS

Unlike most of the surviving blends that based themselves out of London's Docklands, Smith & Cross is a 100% Jamaican rum, as opposed to Demerara rum. The brand has roots that go back as far as 1788, when the company owned blending warehouses and a sugar refinery at 203 Thames Street, not far from the Old Billingsgate market. The blend is cut to Navy Strength (57% ABV) and comprises a mixture of rums sourced from the legendary Hampden Estate in Jamaica's Trelawny parish. Known for its high-ester rums, untamed Hampden can destroy the palates of the uninitiated. Fortunately, Smith & Cross has learned some manners – a six-month-old Wedderburn-style high-ester number paired with an 18–36-month-old medium-bodied Plummer-style rum – and what we're left with is a fantastic Jamaican mixing spirit, perfect for all kinds of funk-driven Tiki concoctions.

THE DUPPY SHARE

One of the biggest new releases of recent years, The Duppy Share has won over both bartenders and consumers with its cute packaging and strong liquid provenance. The brand is the brainchild of George From and Jess Swinfen, and plays off the concept of the angel's share by instead assigning the millions of gallons of evaporative losses that the Caribbean rum industry produces every year to the "duppies" – it's what they call ghosts in Jamaica.

The rum is a blend of 3-year-old Jamaican pot-still rum sourced from Worthy Park, and 5-year-old Barbados column-still rum sourced from the Foursquare distillery. Both rums are matured in ex-bourbon barrels prior to blending.

TORTUGA

Tortuga are a Cayman-based rum blender, named after the legendary isle of Tortuga which contrary to popular belief is not the island of Tortola (one of the British Virgin Islands) but actually a small island off the north coast of Haiti. The bulbous countours of Tortuga were first sighted by Europeans on December 6 1492, when Christopher Columbus saw what looked to be a giant turtle ("tortuga" in Spanish) emerging out of the morning mist.

During the early 17th century, the island was contested on multiple occasions between the Spanish, French and English, and it was probably this constant sense of insecurity that attracted the attentions of pirates and buccaneers. The island became a legendary safe haven for pirates, second only to Port Royal in Jamaica as a criminal trading

BELOW Fabulous packaging and quality liquid – The Duppy Share is everything you can want in a blended rum.

outpost, raiding launchpad, and as a centre for recruitment for the likes of Captain Henry Morgan (see pages 79–81). The gold and loot that flowed through Tortuga was sufficient enough that in the 1660s, the French used Tortuga as the capital of their Sainte-Domingue colony (present-day Haiti).

Tortuga is not a big island (it's about the same size as Marie-Galante), but the green hills in the south known as the "Low Land" were suitable for growing cane, and it's here where the port was located, too. Did the French make rum there? Certainly. But there's little in the way of a surviving record.

Enter the Cayman Islands and the Tortuga Rum Company, which was founded in 1984 by Robert Hamaty and his wife Carlene, an air-hostess. The pair launched Tortuga rum as a novelty item for the growing tourism industry on the island. It is made from a blend of Jamaican pot-still and Barbados rums. It was the launch of Tortuga Rum Cake (a fourth-generation recipe don't y'know…) a few years later that truly changed the business and changed the focus to one of rum-flavoured cake. The company now bakes a range of long-shelflife flavoured cakes on Cayman, Jamaica Barbados and the Bahamas, and exports to all corners of the world.

In 2015 Tortuga's 5-year-old and 12-year-old rums began to be distributed in the US. I can already attest to the popularity of this blended rum among American travellers in Cayman, who return ladened like pack-horses with duty-free cartons of Cayman Island rum.

VELIER

Velier are an independent Italian spirits importer, which happen to specialize in bottling top-quality rum. In a world where whiskies are labeled as "cask strength" or "barrel proof" and even gin is getting the high-strength treatment, rum has lagged behind somewhat. Velier are leading the charge that will change this, through their "Habitation Velier" range, and through other exclusive releases. This is the bleeding edge of rum innovation, and I believe that it is through "pure pot-still" and natural strength rums such as those in the Velier range, that we shall see the rum category mature with dignity over the coming years.

Velier's head-honcho, Luca Gargano, is an unstoppable force who, over the years, has had unprecedented access to rums from some of the great distilleries of old, not to mention new brands from lesser-known operations. Take Caroni for example: a Trinidadian distillery that went silent in 2002, from which Luca acquired casks, bottled them, and pumped life back into a lost brand for an audience of eager rum lovers across the globe. Luca's close relationship wth Yesu Persaud of DDL in Guyana granted him, for some years, exclusive access to some of their oldest and best stocks from the legendary Diamond Distillery. Then there's Velier's work in Haiti, bottling spirits from some of the hardest-to-get-to distilleries on the planet, and ennobling a Haitian craft for spirits that few people would ever have otherwise noticed. Velier's relationship with the Bielle distillery on Marie-Galante has created a partnership that's unheard of between importer and producer, whereby Velier have installed a pot still and now share the pressing equipment in order to make their "Rhum Rhum" brand.

It's no exaggeration whatsoever to suggest that Luca Gargano is the most innovative character in the rum industry today. The products in the Velier range demand a high price tag, but they do so for a very good reason. The Velier liquids are exclusively top-drawer. These are not people who mess about with generic flavours and "safe" blends. They are designed to stand out. They do stand out, in both flavour and in the quality of the packaging – which is among the best clothing you're every likely to see on a bottle of rum. My only real complaint is that the rum all sells out so quickly!

WOOD'S

There are plenty of Black Rum options out there for those with aspirations of joining the Navy or becoming a pirate. All of them rely heavily on the authenticity of their heritage in order to sell their product, and each have their own take on how to approach this subject. Wood's do it the right way, by bottling their rum at 57% ABV, which is the old measure for 100% Imperial proof. In fact, Wood's have been bottling their Demerara rum at this strength for 130 years, during which time it is alleged that the recipe has remained faithful to the original formula too. It seems that the only thing that has changed at all is the packaging.

In fact, the Wood's bottle underwent a significant and much needed redesign in 2016. Prior to this, it was packaged in what is quite literally the cheapest spirit bottle you can buy, complete with flimsy aluminium cap, and jaded label slapped on the front. Not so anymore. The new bottle is a sturdy-looking affair (better suited for rough seas) with a proper cork stopper, and a new cleaned-up label that subtly celebrates the themes of the old bottle while allowing the typography to sing a little louder. It is sure to appeal to the hipster set, at land and at sea. It appeals to me.

The redesign had been on the to-do list for some time of course, as the

ABOVE Authenticity without the cliche – the new label for Wood's Navy rum is a masterclass in product packaging.

Scottish family-run firm William Grant & Sons bought the brand from Seagram's back in 2002. They also snapped up O.V.D. Rum and Vat 19 in the process – the latter being a rum of Trinidadian origin, and the number-one selling aged rum in Northern Ireland at the time. The newly formed tag-team of Wood's and O.V.D (both of them Demerara rums) gave William Grant & Sons a good chunk of the Scottish rum market at the time, which, when coupled with spiced rums, shifts about as many cases in Scotland annually as the entire malt whisky category put together.

The Wood's brand was founded in the Albert Docks in Liverpool, England in 1887. Like many of the companies that got into rum blending, the Wood's Trading Company traded whatever they could to make a quick buck: spying some barrels of Demerara rum on the docks one day, the company saw and opportunity and branched out into rum blending. Lucky they did, since all traces of the original Wood's Trading Company have been lost… only the surviving rum brand serves as testimony of them ever having existed!

The rum is a blend of three stills at the

Diamond distillery: two of them are four-column Savalle stills originating from the Uitvlugt distillery, which closed in 2000 and the other being the Versailles wooden pot still. The rums are matured separately in Guyana then shipped to the UK for bottling. Once the rum lands on British soil, William Grant & Sons perform a marrying process in refill American oak barrels. The rum is rested in these casks for an average of three years (in addition to the maturation the spirit has already undergone in Guyana), but the barrels they use are deliberately very old and exhausted of wood character. The reasoning behind this is that so much character is deemed to come from the Versailles still spirit that it's necessary to further strip out some of the volatile notes through the continued oxidation and evaporation of the spirit.

XM

The XM rum brand is a blend of Guyanese rums. Nothing new there then, except with XM there is one notable point of difference: it's owned by a Guyanese company. Banks DIH (not to be confused with Banks rum) was founded in the 1840s by Jose Gomes D'Aguiar. The DIH in the company name comes from the abbreviation of Demerara Ice House. The company has its roots in rum blending and liquor stores, but it quickly became involved in other areas of trade and commerce. As the company expanded and bought the Demerara Ice House (DIH) which was at the time used to hold the enormous glaciers that were shipped down to Guyana by Canadian schooner – handy if you wanted some ice in your rum. These days, Banks trade across multiple platforms, with shares in banks and shipping companies to their name, as well as the Banks Brewery on Barbados.

Demerara Distillers stand as one of Banks DIH's main competitors, but that doesn't stop them from purchasing rum from them, which they bottle under the XM brand.

The packaging of XM – with its liberal use of airbrushing and raised gold typography – ought to be enough to put people off the brand. The liquid inside is textbook Guyanese, however, and altogether rather difficult to distinguish from the El Dorado range. There's a liberal helping of nutty dessert-like qualities and that present sweet density.

BELOW I'm not a fan of the XM labels, but it's easily forgiven when you get a taste of the rum inside – sweet, forbidden, and altogether rather satisfying.

PART THREE
RUM COCKTAILS

MAI TAI

**55 ML/2 FL. OZ. WRAY & NEPHEW 17-YEAR-OLD SUBSTITUTE BLEND
(SEE BELOW) OR USE EXTRA-AGED POT-STILL RUM**

25 ML/1 FL. OZ. LIME JUICE

10 ML/2 TEASPOONS PIERRE FERRAND DRY ORANGE CURAÇAO

10 ML/2 TEASPOONS ROCK CANDY SYRUP (SEE PAGE 102)

10 ML/2 TEASPOONS ORGEAT

Wray & Nephew 17-year-old substitute blends (mix in equal parts):
For a fruity and spicy Mai Tai: Banks 5-Year-Old and Plantation Original Dark;
For a full-bodied, vegetal Mai Tai: El Dorado 15-Year-Old and Saint James Rhum Vieux;
For an aromatic and waxy Mai Tai: Depaz Hors d'age 2002 Vintage and
Doorly's 12-Year-Old.

You can swizzle this drink straight in the glass if you prefer, but the proper way
is to shake it. Add the ingredients to a cocktail shaker along with 200 g (7 oz.) of
crushed ice. If your ice is a little wet, it's worth putting it through a salad spinner
to dry it out first as this will limit the dilution of the finished drink. Shake well,
then pour the entire contents of the shaker into a large rocks glass. Use the
spent lime shell to garnish the top, and add a sprig of mint to decorate.
Tama'a maita'i!

While it's certain that Mai Tai is one of the great pinups of the Tiki anthology, regrettably this is perhaps the least tropical-tasting drink of this family of tropical-tasting drinks. No pineapple juice, no passionfruit, no grenadine and no coconut – it's enough to make an overproof rum float spontaneously extinguish! In fact, the original version of this drink created by Tiki legend Trader Vic is little more than a Rum-based Margarita or Sidecar with the addition of almond-flavoured syrup. It's the simplicity that makes the drink such a genius concoction and second only to the Daiquiri in rum cocktail fame.

This legendary drink was created by Vic Bergeron in 1944 at the original Soakham branch of Trader Vic's. Bergeron was making drinks for two Tahitian friends, Easham and Carrie Guild, when he combined Wray & Nephew 17 with "fresh lime, some orange curaçao from Holland, a dash of Rock Candy Syrup, and a dollop of French Orgeat, for its subtle almond flavor." This was mixed with "a generous amount of shaved ice and vigorous shaking by hand". The story goes that Carrie Guild took a sip and according to Vic commented "Maita'i Roa A'e", which means "out of this world" or "very good" in Tahitian.

The drink spread throughout Vic's franchised restaurants, and across the US, gobbling up supplies of Wray & Nephew 17 in the process. When stocks of the rum had been depleted, he switched to Wray & Nephew 15, until that began to dry up too. Vic took the decision to stretch out what remaining rum he had by mixing it with Red Heart (which at the time was a Jamaican blend) and Coruba (a Black Rum from Jamaica). By the mid-1950s, Wray & Nephew had been dropped all together, and Vic had turned to a mixture of Jamaican rums combined with *rhum agricole* from Martinique.

Order a Mai Tai these days, and it's usually pot luck as to what you will receive. Some recipes call for bitters, while others use pineapple juice, and more often than not, you'll get an overproof rum float in there too. The original version is by far the best – the only issue being that the legendary Wray & Nephew 17-year-old is no easier to come by now than it was in the 1950s. So just replace it, right? Not so easy. This high-ester pot-still number was the key element that elevated the Mai Tai from the flat and flabby into the sun-drenched realms of Polynesia. There are only a handful of Wray & Nephew 17 bottles still in existence, and most of them are unopened.

I have been lucky enough to taste it in its natural form (thanks Jake Burger), and what a rum it is: with aromas of hot rubber, puffed cereals, tar and freshly greased engine parts. The taste is green peppercorn, bitter artichoke, bitter almond and beef fat. Trader Vic described it as "surprisingly golden in colour, but with a rich and pungent flavour particular to the Jamaican blends". It is/ was a highly stylized spirit, and there are few available rums today that come close to imitating its unique flavour profile, which means that making an authentic tasting Mai Tai in the modern era is no mean feat.

Fortunately for you, I have taken some time to formulate a few blending options that come close to my tasting notes of the original, and they are listed on the previous page. As for the rest of the ingredients, they shouldn't prove too difficult to track down. Rock candy syrup is a supersaturated sugar syrup (or gomme) made by heating two parts sugar with one part water, and allowing to reduce in a pan for five minutes. Once it cools, it should be as viscous as honey.

Try experimenting with different types of sugar (Demerara or light muscovado) for a richer-tasting finished drink. Alternatively, Trader Vic's sell their own branded version of the product.

Victor Bergeron, the founder of Trader Vic's, in the original Trader Vic's bar in Oakland, California.

MOJITO

12 FRESH MINT LEAVES
50 ML/1⅓ FL. OZ. HAVANA CLUB 3-YEAR-OLD
20 ML/1 FL. OZ. LIME JUICE
10 ML/2 TEASPOONS SUGAR SYRUP (SEE PAGE 102)
SODA

Judging by the number of bad Mojitos I've been served in my time, this is not an easy drink to balance. The mistake that many bartenders make is muddling/crushing whole wedges of lime into the drink. This is a poor tactic, because limes vary dramatically in the amount of juice they offer up, and unless the sugar is balanced accordingly, you'll be landed with something that's insipidly sweet or far too sour. The peel on the lime is better avoided too – it's quite a potent flavour that tends to mask the cool aromatics of the mint.

Take a chunky highball and throw the mint leaves in there. Please don't "slap" them as is the ritual of some cocktail makers – in doing so you're merely aromatizing your hands. Gently bruise the mint leaves using a muddler (a rolling pin works fine, too). It's essential that you're gentle – if you crush the leaves you'll release bitter-tasting chlorophyll into the drink. Douse the leaves in the rum and give a good stir, then add the lime juice and sugar syrup. Throw a scoop of crushed ice in there (you can use cubed, but crushed ice will give a far better appearance) and give the mixture a good "churn" with a long spoon. Pile more ice on top, give it another stir, then fill any space with soda. Stir again, add more ice (if needed) then garnish with a lime wedge and a fresh sprig of mint. Drink with a straw.

There aren't many drinks that speak to rum so much as the Mojito. It's packaged Cuban mojo; the perfect antidote to the heady spice of a fine Cuba cigar. A liquid embodiment of all that is sprightly, fresh and spirited.

The earliest reference to the Mojito was in Sloppy Joe's Havana Bar, which were giving away a souvenir cocktail pamphlet in 1931 with the recipe. Those

of you who are well-read when it comes to cocktail history will be aware that the pamphlet actually listed two versions of the drink: one under "Bacardí Cocktails"; and another under "Gordon's Gin Cocktails". The latter, of course, uses a base of gin in place of rum, and the former is based on Bacardí, which is essentially the same drink we make today (though it won't be with Bacardí if you're drinking it in Havana). The dual versions were again offered up in the legendary El Floridita's cocktail book, published in 1939, which offered a Mojito Criollo #1 (with rum) and Mojito Criollo #2 (with gin). These twin faces of the Mojito have led some bar historians to suggest that the original cocktail was actually based on an American drink called the "Southside".

The timings do indeed make this a possibility, because the earliest story to mention the Southside comes from the Southside Sportsmen's Club in Long Island, during the 1890s. Fizzes were very much on-trend back then, and through the actions of some adventurous bartender, mint leaves appeared in a Gin Fizz one day, and thus the Southside was born.

If it sounds simple, that's because it is. So simple in fact, that the mixture of lime, water, booze and mint has in fact been going on for far longer than than either the Southside or the Mojito. The earliest known example of this is really an early form of Navy Grog, which was named El Draque, after the Spanish nickname for the British privateer Francis Drake. Made from *aguardiente de caña*, lime, sugar and mint, this fiery mix would likely have been closer to a Ti Punch (see pages 114–15) than a Mojito, but clearly cut from the same cloth. Whether Drake actually drank one of these things is questionable, since he lived in the late-16th century, a time when cane spirits were difficult to come across outside Brazil. Plus, it seems an incredible coincidence that one of the greatest explorers of his time was also the world's first mixologist. But if indeed he did have a hand to play in the drink's conception, El Draque has a fair claim to being the world's oldest cocktail.

However it was invented, the drink became very popular among the Cuban peasantry in the early 1800s, some 90 years before the Southside or the Daiquiri (see pages 112–13) – another drink it is claimed to spawn from – were invented. It was also in the second quarter of the 19th century that El Draque turns up (as the "Draquecito") in *El Colera en la Habana*, a story by Cuban poet/novelist Ramón de Palma.

The etymology of the Mojito is not entirely clear. It could come from the Spanish word *mojadito* (meaning "a little wet"), or it might have evolved from a recipe for "Mojo" – a lime- and mint-based salsa.

Blanche Z. De Baralt's *Cuban Cookery: Gastronomic Secrets of the Tropics, with an Appendix on Cuban Drinks* (1931) included a recipe for "Rum Cocktail (Cuban Mojo)" and directions to make what is quite clearly a Mojito.

If La Floridita is the cradle of the Daiquiri, it's Old Havana's La Bodeguita Del Medio where the Mojito rests its head (Hemingway was once known to pen words to the same effect). This modest little boozer was a latecomer to the Havana bar scene when farmer Angel Martinez opened it on Calle Empedrado in 1942. The bar soon established a reputation among the locals for its unassuming style and was visited by luminaries including Hemingway and Pablo Neruda. These days it's characterized by decades' worth of handwritten messages on the walls, and the fact that the bartenders here mechanically churn out up to a dozen Mojitos a minute. If that kind of product volume doesn't flash warning signs at you, let me make it crystal clear for you: if it's a great drink you're after, La Bodeguita del Medio is better avoided.

As is the unfortunate norm with cocktails and the bars that originate

them, a thriving tourism trade has done away with any suggestion of quality that may (or may not) have once existed here. Pre-packaged lime juice, mint stalks and overzealous measures of Havana Club 3-Year-Old are the themes that populate my all-too-hazy memories of the experience.

CUBA LIBRE

50 ML/1⅔ FL. OZ. AGED WHITE RUM

120 ML/4 FL. OZ. COCA-COLA

HALF A LIME

In accordance with the version of this drink in Charles H. Baker's *Gentleman's Companion* (1939), I'm a strong advocate of a quick lime muddle as the first step of construction. Squeeze the lime juice into a separate vessel, and drop the spent shell into a highball glass. Squash it to remove the oils, then add cubed ice, rum, lime juice and coke. Give it a good stir, and add more ice or coke if desired. Substitute the aged white rum for a white overproof rum (such as Bacardi 151) and the drink becomes a "Cuban Missile Crisis"!

Sometimes the simplest drinks are the best. In fact, more often than not the simplest drinks are the best. This is certainly true of the Cuba Libre, which comprises only two ingredients plus a very necessary garnish. Some would argue this isn't a cocktail at all, but a spirit and mixer. But those folks fail to recognize the genius of Coca-Cola as a bittersweet ingredient and the complexity of its composition.

A quick scan over the key flavours of Coca-Cola: lemon, orange, lime, cinnamon, nutmeg, neroli, lavender and coriander/cilantro; shows a set of ingredients that match nicely with rum as stand-alone modifiers. Indeed, most of them have coupled historically with rum in punches and other cocktails. What all this means is that the affinity between rum and coke is a favourable accident – there is something at work here that blends these flavours into something unnaturally tasty.

So where did it come from? Well, the Cuba Libre ("Free Cuba") is named of

course for the Cuban War of Independence, which was fought from 1895–98. We can be sure that this drink didn't exist in Cuba prior to this, because Coca-Cola wasn't available there until after the war, and not bottled for export until 1899. The year of the birth of the Cuba Libre cocktail is cited as 1900, and in an unprecedented turn of events, this was sworn under a legal affidavit by a man named Fausto Rodriguez in 1960. Rodriguez was a messenger with the US Army Signal Corps who claimed to have walked to a Havana bar in 1900 and bore witness to an officer by the name of Captain Russell, ordering a Bacardi and Coca-Cola on ice with a wedge of lime. More soldiers arrived and a second round was ordered, to which the bartenders suggested a toast of ¡Por Cuba Libre! to celebrate of the newly liberated Cuba.

It later transpired that Rodriguez was on the Bacardi payroll and that the affidavit only came to light as a result of a full-age advertisement in Life magazine taken out by Bacardi in 1966. For what it's worth, I suspect the story has some truth to it. But as for the brand, well, that's anyone's guess.

Whatever the origins, the drink travelled north, into the US, and quickly became popular among the Cola-guzzling southerners. By 1920 there were 1,000 Coca-Cola bottling plants (compared to two in 1900) and rum was the go-to adulterator. This practice was sustained during Prohibition, as Caribbean rum was one of the few spirits that found its way across US border. The Cuba Libre became the most dependable beverage, especially during wartime, when sugar and other sodas were rationed. During World War II, coke was distributed among soldiers, so there was always a plentiful supply to mix with the steady influx of rum.

The drink's celebrity status was confirmed once and for all in 1945 with the popular calypso hit "Rum and Coca-Cola" by the Andrews Sisters. As a trio of sisters from Minnesota, the Andrews had to put on faux-Caribbean accents in order to hit the correct calypso vibe. The melody had been previously published as the work of Trinidadian calypso composer Lionel Belasco on a song titled "L'Année Passée," which was in turn based on a folk song from Martinique. The lyrics to "Rum and Coca-Cola" were provided by Rupert Grant, another calypso musician from Trinidad who went by the stage name Lord Invader, and it was he who adjusted the song to reference the off-duty activities of American soldiers.

The song was a massive hit among the locals, despite the allusion to prostitution, the glorification of drinking and free advertising for Coca-Cola. Perhaps it was the transformative nature of the song, with its weird lyrics and kooky accents. Maybe it was just the fact that rum and coke is a fantastic drink.

Since the Yankee come to Trinidad
They got the young girls all goin' mad
Young girls say they treat 'em nice
Make Trinidad like paradise

Drinkin' rum and Coca-Cola
Go down Point Koo-mah-nah
Both mother and daughter.
Workin' for the Yankee dollar

The Andrews Sisters pose for a portrait around 1944 in New York City.

DARK AND STORMY

120 ML/2 FL. OZ. LUSCOMBE ORGANIC "HOT" GINGER BEER
50 ML/1⅔ FL. OZ. GOSLINGS BLACK SEAL RUM
WEDGE OF LIME

Build the drink into a highball glass filled with plenty of ice.

Unlike most cocktails, it's nice to take a backwards approach and add the rum to the glass last, along with a squashed wedge of lime. This means you get the full effect of the "storm" as the light and heavy liquids fight to remain separate. Some people add a dash of Angostura Bitters and a sprig of mint, moving the cocktail more in the direction of a Moscow Mule, but if your ginger beer is good enough, there really is no need for further distractions.

There are only a handful of cocktails on the planet that are legally trademarked, and for reasons unknown, all but one of them (the Sazerac) is based on rum. No prizes for guessing that the Bacardi Cocktail (a Daiquiri with grenadine) is one of them; less obvious is the Painkiller (see pages 126-27) and less desirable is the Hand Grenade (a sweet punch served in nasty little green plastic "hand grenades" from late-night bars in New Orleans), and then there's the rather appealing Dark 'n' Stormy.

Yes sir, this drink – which is made using Gosling's Black Seal rum, ginger beer and, occasionally, lime juice – has been under the stewardship of Gosling Brothers in Bermuda since it first manifested itself around the time of World War I. The flavour pairing has more distant origins (which we'll come on to) and of course you're free to call a dark rum and ginger whatever you like, but if you're using the name Dark 'n' Stormy) (or Dark & Stormy) on a

cocktail menu or even in a book, you are legally obliged to use Gosling's in the recipe.

This is no great hardship, as Black Seal is a benchmark blend featuring high-ester Jamaican rum and sweet-lingering Guyanese, topped off with a good slug of spirit caramel for added effect (for more on Gosling's, see pages 82-83). Gosling's first trademarked the drink in the late 1970s, and since then, Bermuda has become the unofficial home of the drink. Its spiritual home is of course, at sea, which makes Bermuda as good a choice as any since it's nearly 1,000 km (620 miles) from the nearest landmass.

By the late 19th century, the spice trade on some Caribbean islands, like Grenada, had surpassed that of sugar. Merchant sailors, who plied their trade between the sticky ports of the Caribbean and the British Isles, would regularly transport shipments of rum alongside their spices. These spices appealed to blenders, who used them to

flavour their rums, but they were also used to make sodas and medicinal tonics too. Ginger beer really was the flavour of Victorian Britain, and just like tea, it was a celebration of the British Empire's conquests abroad. The British Royal Navy took a keen interest in the stuff and began provisioning ginger beer on board their ships. Perhaps it was an attempt to curb alcoholism among the ship's crew, or to help with sea sickness, or maybe it even served as a heartening taste of home – either way it was popular enough that between 1860 and 1920 the Royal Navy Dockyard on Ireland Island (in Bermuda) even had its own ginger beer bottling plant. And even though there's no documented evidence to prove it, I don't think it's too much of a stretch to suggest that one or two sailors dipped a toe into the water and experimented with mixing their rum ration with ginger beer.

Back in London, the city was awash with ginger beer, with street vendors on every corner peddling their own unique recipes. One of them, William John Barritt, came to Bermuda from England and in 1874 opened a dry goods shop on the corner of Front and King Streets in Hamilton, Bermuda. This is where the Bermuda's now-famous Barritt's Ginger Beer first started. Even today, after five generations, it's still going strong.

Gosling's themselves have dabbled in ginger beer called "Gosling's Stormy Ginger Beer", which is touted as "the only ginger beer created strictly to make Dark 'n' Stormy cocktails". It's alright stuff, but finer specimens can be found if you hunt around.

My preference lies with the bottle-fermented kind, such as the one made by Luscombe, a soft drinks company based in Devon, England. This location is well-suited to the task because Devon, after all, is the birthplace of the word "rumbullion" (see page 21). More important than that is the flavour of the product, which is outstanding. It comes in two different temperatures: "cool" and "hot". I prefer the "hot", which induces a sufficient volume of sweat to have you believe you're sailing in very warm waters. With its densely concentrated, almost chewy, texture, this disturbingly opaque beer is more than a match for the richness of Gosling's Black Seal.

As for the name "Dark 'n' Stormy", well that was likely chosen on account of the drink's brooding appearance when mixed. Dark clouds of alcohol and spice engulf each other in an altogether discomforting fashion. But the term "Dark and Stormy" may in itself have been borrowed from *Paul Clifford*, a successful novel of 1830 by Edward Bulwer-Lytton. The novel's opening paragraph begins, "It was a dark and stormy night; the rain fell in torrents", and is often invoked as the archetypal example of melodramatic prose in fiction writing.

"It was a dark and stormy night; the rain fell in torrents"
Paul Clifford (1830) by Edward Bulwer-Lytton

DAIQUIRI

60 ML/2 FL. OZ. BACARDI CARTA BLANCA
15 ML/½ FL. OZ. FRESH LIME JUICE
10 ML/2 TEASPOONS SUGAR SYRUP (SEE PAGE 102)

Add all the ingredients to a cocktail shaker and shake vigorously with
cubed ice for at least 30 seconds. Strain into a frozen coupe glass.
Don't garnish it – there's no point – the drink will be gone before you
(or your guests) even notice it's there.

During the course of the Spanish-American War in 1898, thousands of acres of Cuban sugar plantations passed into American ownership. US control over mining also expanded, and this resulted in a huge influx of expatriated American workers to Cuba in the latter years of the 19th century. Jennings Cox was one such man, an American mining engineer who in 1896 worked for the Spanish-American Iron Company, near the village of Daiquirí (correctly pronounced dai-ki-REE), close to Santiago de Cuba. Conditions in the Sierra Maestra region of Cuba was tough (yellow fever was highly prevalent) and the workers were compensated (in part) with tobacco and Bacardi Carta Blanca rum rations.

The story goes that Cox was entertaining some friends with cocktails one evening when he ran out of gin. Not wishing to end the party early, he called upon a bottle of Bacardi rum, serving it mixed with sugar, "lemons" and water, and pouring it into a tall glass filled with ice. The recipe for this "Daiquiri" was recorded by Mr. Cox on a handwritten sheet of paper. There are

some obvious discrepancies between Cox's original formula and the standard accepted Daiquiri of today. Most notable is that the drink was served long, but with the simultaneous rise of the Martini in the early 20th century, the drink seems to have shifted allegiances to the coupe glass. Cox's version also calls for lemon juice instead of lime, but there's a little more to this than meets the eye. Limes were far more common in Cuba than lemons at that time (they still are) and were known to Cubans as limón, so it's quite likely that what Cox was really referring to was a lime after all. While the above creation story seems the most credible, there are many others that place American military officers and even Don Facundo Bacardí Masso at the crime scene (who presumably appeared as a ghostly aspiration since he died in 1886). All of this, of course, is slightly fatuous, as, if you'll allow me to quote myself in *The Curious Bartender: The Artistry & Alchemy of Creating the Perfect Cocktail* (2013):

"It doesn't take a mining engineer to work out that a drink as simple as this probably pre-dates Jennings Cox, albeit

under different titles. Surely many a rum punch has existed containing only rum, lime, sugar and water? – and you only need to look at the Brazilian Caipirinha to see a cousin of the Daiquiri, comprising much the same ingredients all served over ice."

The Daiquiri is not a forgiving cocktail when it comes to subtle changes in its formula, and one of the things that really rattles me when it comes to the Daiquiri, is when it is confused with a Sour. Now, the sour family of cocktails are a simple bunch: four parts spirit, two parts citrus, one part sugar – you can't go wrong really. A proper Daiquiri cannot be made like this though, as the light, Cuban-style rum is easily overshadowed

by all that sweet and sour. This cocktail is about discretion and finesse, and to balance it correctly, you need a higher ratio of rum: eight parts rum, one part lime, and just over one part sugar (depending on how sweet your sugar syrup is). With this formula, the drink is less opaque, and seems to glow with a soft turquoise luminance. It tastes far better too, as those soft *aguardiente* notes are gently sweetened, penetrating through fleshy citrus with grace. Also, the subtle sourness means you can skull three of them in quick succession and not experience that puffy mouth feeling that comes from one too many sweet and sour cocktails.

TI PUNCH

**50 ML/1⅔ FL. OZ. BIELLE PREMIUM BLANC (ANY RHUM AGRICOLE
WILL DO BUT THIS IS ONE OF MY FAVOURITES)
SMALL WEDGE OF LIME
1 SMALL TEASPOON BROWN SUGAR**

Add the lime to a small rocks glass and gently squash with the back of a spoon.
Next add the rum and the sugar. Give everything a good stir until all the sugar
has dissolved. If you prefer, you can make a sugar syrup (see page 102) and
forgo all of the stirring, but the French tend to opt for granulated sugar,
which draws out more of the lime oils.

The Ti Punch (pronounced tee-pawnch) is a drink that hails from the French islands of the West Indies, and is synonymous with the drinking of the local *rhum agricole*. This "little punch", as it translates to is, in many ways, more than a mixed drink or a cocktail. For many, it's the final stage in the making of the rum, as if the liquid in the bottle was never intended to be served "as-is", but to be seasoned with a squeeze of lime, carefully sweetened with a spoon of sugar, then stirred, sipped and enjoyed.

It's customary not to use ice in a Ti Punch which, when coupled with the typically high strength of *rhum agricole*, makes for a fiery little drink that's packed full of flavour. It's for this reason that folks probably decided to make them nice and compact. Some, indeed, can be laughably small – barely a mouthful. My friend Patricia, who lives in Pointe-à-Pitre, Guadeloupe, would make Ti Punches in tiny blue glasses hardly bigger than an egg cup. The drink would be consumed within a couple of minutes, and then she would return to

the ritual of muddling the tiny lime slice and slowly dissolving the sugar into the rum. And it is perhaps this ritual of squashing, spooning, pouring and stirring, that makes it such an evocative drink to enjoy. Pound for pound it's one of the most arduous drinks to put together, but much like a shot of espresso, the reward is certainly worth it.

If you go into a bar in the French Caribbean and order a Ti Punch, more often than not they will serve you an entire bottle of rum, lime wedges, sugar and an empty glass, then invite you to mix your own. This means you can get your hands dirty and easily tweak the proportions to your own preferred levels of strength, sourness and sweetness. It also means things can quickly escalate, as half a bottle of 50% liquor vanishes in a matter of minutes. In these circumstances, the bartender will gauge how much of the bottle has gone and charge you accordingly. By that point you're happy to go along with anything.

Making a Ti Punch is as easy as it gets, and a great backup plan for when you

run out of ice. The golden rule is that you must use *rhum agricole*, but as far as the other parts go it's your choice as to whether you use lemon or lime, and white sugar or brown. My preference lies with the latter in both cases. If you prefer, you can use a *vieux* (aged) rum, but I think this drink is better suited to the feral aromatics of *agricole blanc*.

PLANTER'S PUNCH

400 G/14 OZ. DARJEELING TEA
120 G/4¼ OZ. DEMERARA SUGAR
3 G/¹⁄₁₆ OZ. SALT
150 ML/5 FL. OZ. LIME JUICE
50 ML/1²⁄₃ FL. OZ. GRAPEFRUIT JUICE
300 ML/10 FL. OZ. AGED POT-STILL RUM

(makes 1 litre/34 fl. oz.)

Start by brewing the tea (nice and strong) and while it cools, dissolve the sugar
and salt into it. Juice your citrus fruits, strain out the pulp, and mix with the
rum. Once the tea has cooled, mix everything together, pop it in a bottle,
and leave in the fridge until needed (it will keep for up to two weeks).
Simply pour over ice cubes to serve.

Punches pre-date cocktails by at least 200 years and form the basis of the sour and fizz cocktail families. Some punches are quite specific in their recipes, while others are a touch more conceptual; Planter's Punch certainly falls into the latter category. It's been known as "Jamaican Rum Punch" in *The Savoy Cocktail Book* and referred to as "Creole Punch" by the British novelist Alec Waugh, and it probably started its life as a mixture of pot-still rum, citrus, sugar and water.

Nowadays it's not uncommon to find folk adding liqueurs, grenadine, orange juice or passion fruit to a Planter's Punch. On this one occasion I would advocate a *carte-blanche* approach to your punch- making. So long as you stick by the classic ratio of "two of sour, one of sweet, three of strong (rum) and four of weak," you pretty much can't go wrong.

You'll know if it's worked, because you'll experience an irrepressible desire to go back for a second or third glass. This is the whole point of punch – a convivial drink that would look absurd if served in a large glass, but positively tragic if offered only once and in a small quantity. Of course, the effect might not be instantaneous, as writer Patrick Chamoiseau reminds us: "a rum punch takes a good six hours to penetrate the soul. Six hours, between the midday punch that wards off the sun's madness and the push before your evening soup, the commander of your dreams."

In the past, punches were made with a type of sugar known as "loaf sugar", which was named for the fact that you bought it in tall loaves that look a bit like missile warheads. The shape was on account of the earthenware moulds into which the molten sugar was poured for setting. Loaf sugar was graded for quality, with white stuff (not dissimilar to our modern-day table sugar) reserved only for

the well-off. Most folks could only afford a loaf that sat somewhere in the realms of light muscovado or Demerara sugar, which was no bad thing as far as the punch bowl was concerned, because these sugars offered up flavour as well as sweetness.

As for the rum itself, this is not the occasion to shy away from flavour. Punch and rum co-existed in an age of British pot-still liquid stink. A slight "grottiness" to your punch therefore only heightens the authenticity of the beverage.

PIÑA COLADA

25 ML/1 FL. OZ. DON Q CRISTAL WHITE
25 ML/1 FL. OZ. BACARDI 8-YEAR-OLD
**50 ML/1⅔ FL. OZ. PRESSURE-COOKED COCONUT MILK
(CAN BE SUBSTITUTED FOR THE REGULAR STUFF)**
60 ML/2 FL. OZ. PRESSED PINEAPPLE JUICE
10 ML/2 TEASPOONS LIME JUICE
0.5 G/PINCH OF SALT

Add all the ingredients to a blender along with 100 g/3½ oz. of ice (per serving).
Blitz it for a good 30 seconds, or until it's silky smooth and lump-free.
Serve immediately in a hurricane glass (you know the one, it's like an elongated
wine glass with a short stem) with a straw, and garnish with a wedge of
pineapple and a fresh cherry.

If it were possible to bottle the concentrated flavour of a holiday by the beach, it would probably taste something like a Piña Colada. Little wonder that sunscreen manufacturers borrow the classic combination of pineapple and coconut to aromatize their products. Hell, the Piña Colada even looks like a holiday, and a lazy one at that – quietly content as it wallows in its cool and gloopy state, all ludicrous in its bulging proportions and ostentatious garnishing. If Piña Colada were a vehicle, it would be a carnival float. If it were a person, it would lounge by the pool in a skin-tight, leopard-print swimming thong to match its day-glow tan and moustache. There are only two types of people in the world: those who love a Piña Colada, and those who don't admit to loving them. You see, it's ok to be a holiday drink, so long as you treat it with some respect – the golden rule being that you

shouldn't drink Piña Colada on a weekly, or even monthly basis. This is for the same reasons that it's impractical to take a vacation every week – you'll put on weight, won't be able to hold down a job and your friends will laugh at you.

No, the Piña Colada is far more a dessert that happens to contain alcohol than a mixed drink; a guilty pleasure when nobody is looking. After all, a single glass can often contain the same amount of calories as a cheeseburger, only without the associated stigma of ordering a second burger. Indeed, given the right conditions, a decent Piña Colada can slip down with surprising ease, with the rum passing by almost completely undetected. It's a WMD in disguise, but not just from an alcohol standpoint. If you put away three or four of them quickly, you may find your hands trembling from the hyperglycemia. Next comes the "crash" and that's followed up by a side serving of Type 2 Diabetes.

I jest, of course. For many people the Piña Colada is the definitive cocktail – one that best represents the glitzy vulgarity of 1980s Tom Cruise bartending. Nostalgia like that is a difficult sentiment to shatter, no matter how impractical the drink may be.

The good news is that it's laughably easy to make, and requires only three ingredients (rum, coconut milk and pineapple juice), along with ice and a blender. Of course, if you have access to a "slushy" machine, all the better. That's how they make them these days at Barrachina, in San Juan, Puerto Rico, where the drink was purportedly invented. Hordes of tourists rock up to this joint every day, and the staff rapidly churn out the cocktail at the peculiarly exacting price of $7.81 (£6.30) a piece. The drink's inventor – Ramón Portas Mingot – created it at Barrachina in 1963, although that recipe also included condensed milk. Like most drinks, the claim is contested, by another Ramón as it happens: Ramón Marrero. He was allegedly working at San Juan's Caribe Hilton in 1954 when he created the drink. One thing that both gentlemen can agree on is that the inventor was called Ramón.

The creation of the drink was only made possible thanks to the arrival of the Coco López brand of coconut cream, launched in Puerto Rico in 1948. The Piña Colada is now the national drink of Puerto Rico and is celebrated on National Piña Colada day, on July 10.

The classic Piña Colada formula calls for light rum, pineapple juice and cream of coconut. It's too sweet and too light on the rum to my tastes, so I suggest using a combination of light and dark rums, and cutting back on the pineapple slightly.

For bonus points, you can "pimp your piña" by popping the sealed can of coconut milk in a pressure cooker set to maximum temperature for an hour or so. This kickstarts Maillard (browning) reactions, as the sugars and enzymes go to work on each other, which results in a toasted, biscuity, almost buttery, coconut milk that makes the normal stuff seem bland. Don't skimp on the pineapple juice, make sure you buy the best stuff you can find and sweeten according to your taste, which for me means barely sweetening at all.

HURRICANE

60 ML/2 FL. OZ. AGED BLENDED RUM
25 ML/1 FL. OZ. FRESH ORANGE JUICE
15 ML/½ FL. OZ. FRESH LIME JUICE
**25 ML/1 FL. OZ. PASSIONFRUIT SYRUP (STORE-BOUGHT
STUFF TENDS TO BE QUITE GOOD)**
10 ML/2 TEASPOONS GRENADINE (SEE BELOW)

Add all the ingredients to a cocktail shaker filled with ice. Shake for 10 seconds,
then strain into a rocks glass (or Hurricane glass) filled with ice.
Garnish with a pineapple leaf.

GRENADINE

500 G/17½ OZ. CASTER/SUPERFINE SUGAR
500 ML/17½ FL. OZ. WATER
200 G/7 OZ. POMEGRANATE SEEDS
200 G/7 OZ. RASPBERRIES
2 G/½ TEASPOON SALT
(makes approx 1 kg/34 fl. oz.)

Add all the ingredients to a plastic zip-lock bag and pop it into a pot of hot
water set at 50°C/122°F (or alternately use a sous vide water bath). Keep a
constant temperature of around 50°C/122°F for 4 hours, then carefully strain
the ingredients through a mesh sieve/strainer. If you're planning on storing
your grenadine (in the fridge) for more than a week, it's worth adding
100 ml/3½ fl. oz. of vodka to the finished syrup, as this doubles its shelf life.

The Hurricane is probably the biggest
and silliest member of the entire Tiki
family. But it's an important drink, as it
lends its name to glassware which goes
by the same name, which is also used to
serve drinks like the Piña Colada and
Zombie.

The unlikely home of this drink is Pat
O'Brien's Irish bar in New Orleans's
French Quarter. New Orleans is
probably home to more classic cocktails
than any other city in the world, with
the possible exception of New York and
London. Present day New Orleans is a
curious mixture of colonial French
dining rooms, wood-panelled grand
hotels, sticky-floored karaoke joints and
all-night dive bars. The infamous

Bourbon Street is at the centre of all this: a long and grotty strip of neon debauchery, masking the greatest bars in the history of the American cocktail.

But some of these bars are greater than others. In the case of Pat O'Brien's, we have as abstract an interpretation of the Irish bar concept as you're likely to find.

The bar allegedly started as a speakeasy with the not-at-all-suspect sounding name of "Mr. O'Brien's Club Tipperary". The password to gain entry was "storm's brewin". After Prohibition, Pat explored various ways to rid himself of all the low-quality rum that had been smuggled into New Orleans during the 1920s. The story goes that Mr. O'Brien mixed a few ingredients together (rum, lime, orange and passionfruit) and marketed it to sailors by serving it in a glass that was the same shape as a hurricane lamp.

The popularity of the drink grew, and with it so too did the bar. Pat O'Brien's now occupies an old colonial property just off Bourbon Street, but the merriment spills into a paved rear courtyard with its flaming fountains and garish green lighting. The tacky lights will do little to detract your attention from your drink however – as is so often the case with bars whose drinks become more famous than they are, it's the direst possible interpretation of the drink that you're presented with.

A Pat O'Brien's Hurricane is one of the great wonders of the modern world; the colour of glacé/candied cherry and the size of a small leg. Don't order one unless you have an empty stomach, because it's positively rammed full of sugar and artificial flavours. Most people don't have the stamina or the inclination to finish one – if you have any sense of self-worth, I would implore you not to. The Hurricane is widely recognized as a strong drink, and while the New Orleans original may contain a lot of alcohol, in this instance it is completely overshadowed by fruit juice and syrups. A Pat O'Brien's Hurricane is a regrettable meal in a glass; like a dozen melted popsicles fortified with bad rum. But Pat O'Brien's has made a serious business off the back of flogging these things, both in the bar, as well as in powdered sachets of "Pat O'Brien's Hurricane mix" – perfect for reliving the abomination in the comfort of your own home. Pat O'Brien's even bottle their own rum (so you don't need to waste a decent brand in the drink). It really is rare to see a bar capitalize so completely on the association of a single drink.

For my version of the Hurricane, I've kept things simple and made the drink a little shorter, so it's more like a long Daiquiri modified with passionfruit and pomegranate. The drink is traditionally prepared with a blend of aged and un-aged rums, but if you're careful about selecting the right rum in the first instance, I think you can get by just fine with only one. You can substitute the homemade grenadine for a store-bought option, but it's really worth going to the effort making your own grenadine, as the commercially available options are awful.

EL PRESIDENTE

50 ML/1⅔ FL. OZ. AGED BLENDED RUM
35 ML/1¼ FL. OZ. DOLIN BLANC VERMOUTH DE CHAMBÉRY
5 ML/1 TEASPOON PIERRE FERRAND DRY ORANGE CURAÇAO

Stir the ingredients together over cubed ice, then strain into a chilled coupe glass.

An altogether under-recognized and under-ordered cocktail, El Presidente is a lost treasure from the golden age of the Cuban Club de Cantineros. It was invented in Havana at some point during American Prohibition and probably named for Gerado Machado – a man who would score a B+ on the Latin American dictator brutality scale – who served as president from 1925 to 1933. Many historians point to Eddie Woelke, an American bartender at the Jockey Club in Havana for the creation of both the El Presidente and the Mary Pickford cocktail (rum, pineapple, maraschino and grenadine).

The drink later became the house serve at Club El Chico in New York's Greenwich village, which was run by Spanish immigrant Benito Collada. Following prohibition, El Chico had its own brand of Cuban rum bottled for use in the drink. In 1949, *Esquire's Handbook for Hosts* commented: "The vanguard of Manhattan cognoscenti has discovered what regulars of El Chico in the Village have known for many a moon: the El Presidente cocktail is elixir for jaded gullets."

For many, El Presidente is rum's answer to a Manhattan or Rob Roy cocktail (whisky, vermouth and bitters) but once you get to know the drink intimately, you come to realize that it sits in a family of cocktails all of its own. There are no bitters for a start, instead we have orange curaçao and occasionally grenadine as modifiers. But the fact that both of these ingredients are quite sweet, and the fact that rum and vermouth are both prone to wander into sweetness too, means that El Presidente is a drink that's prone to differ enormously depending on who's got their hands on the barspoon.

The 1935 *La Floridita Cocktail Book* lists the drink simply as equal parts Bacardi Oro (gold), and Vermouth Chambéry, with a teaspoon of orange curaçao. It's stirred over ice and garnished with a cherry and orange zest. The important distinction here is the use of blanc vermouth de Chambéry, which is a colourless, sweet vermouth style, that's more herb-centric and less spicy than Italian rosso vermouth. It was originally commercialized by Chambéry producer Dolin, who have an Appellation d' Origine Contrôlée (AOC) designation on the style.

Later versions of the drink increased the quantity of curaçao and threw in some grenadine, which might have been an effort to combat the less sweet "dry" vermouths that became popular in the

mid-20th century.

It just so happens that the original recipe (very nearly) got it right, so assuming you can get your hands on a blanc vermouth, you needn't worry about the grenadine at all. For my tastes, I do prefer to drop the ratio of vermouth ever-so-slightly, however.

PAINKILLER

50 ML/1⅔ FL. OZ. PUSSER'S RUM
50 ML /1⅔ FL. OZ. PRESSED PINEAPPLE JUICE
25 ML/1 FL. OZ. CREAMED COCONUT
10 ML/2 TEASPOONS FRESH ORANGE JUICE
5 ML/1 TEASPOON SUGAR SYRUP (SEE PAGE 102)

Add all the ingredients to a cocktail shaker and shake with cubed ice.
Next, dump the ice and shake the cocktail again (with no ice) – this has
the effect of "fluffing" the drink up a bit, lightening the texture. The same
can also be achieved with a handheld milk frother, or even a blender.
Pour into a highball glass and garnish with a dusting of ground
cinnamon and nutmeg.

Just like the Dark 'n' Stormy (see pages
109–111), the Painkiller is one of a select
breed of cocktails that has been awarded
a trademark. The trademark belongs to
Pusser's (more about them on pages
91–92), who will send the Feds round to
your house if you even dream of using a
different rum brand to make your
"killer" part of this cocktail. On paper
the drink is not a world away from a
Piña Colada. But unlike the Piña Colada,
it's built rather than blended, and topped
off with a dusting of cinnamon and
nutmeg as a garnish. It's these slight
deviations from the Piña Colada, along
with the richness of the rum required,
that transforms a leisurely ride on a
pleasure boat into a perilous journey
though treacherous waters.

At times, I have wondered if the
inventor of the Painkiller misplaced a
comma in the drink's name, because
"Pain, Killer" would be a more fitting
description. Once, during a notably

masochistic session of Painkiller
consumption, with some Australians in a
beach bar in Cane Garden Bay on the
British Virgin Islands, which has for
better or worse designated itself as the
holy keeper of the Painkiller – I returned
to my lodgings in high spirits. Little did
I know that the alcohol content was
considerably higher than I had expected,
so high in fact that I was bedridden for
the better part of the whole of the
following day. That was the "pain" part.
The "killer" blow happened when I
found myself back in the same bar the
same day ordering another Painkiller.

The problem, as with all the world's
most dangerous drinks, is the apparent
ease at which these things slide down. It
is a trait of the Tiki movement for sure,
but the Painkiller is the grand master.
For many people, a great cocktail is one
that successfully conceals the alcohol. I
wholly disagree with this; good
integration of alcohol into a drink can

focus flavour and lengthen finish, balance sweetness, and serve as a welcome reminder to slow down. But if we were to grade cocktails on their ability to conceal booze, the Painkiller would be up there with the best of them.

My version of this drink is shorter than the classic, taking it further away from Piña Colada territory and more into the realms of Treacle (see pages 128–9). You will find that the subtle heat from the alcohol is a welcome addition, and that the concentrated flavour of pineapple interplays nicely with the spices. If you prefer to make the classic version, I advise a ratio of 2:1:1:1 in favour of the pineapple juice. Whatever you do, be sure to use the best-quality pineapple juice that you can get your hands on.

TREACLE

50 ML/1⅔ FL. OZ. AGED POT-STILL RUM
20 ML/⅔ FL. OZ. APPLE JUICE (FROM CONCENTRATE)
10 ML/2 TEASPOONS SUGAR SYRUP (SEE PAGE 102)
2 DASHES OF ANGOSTURA BITTERS

Add all the ingredients to a rocks glass with a large scoop of cubed ice.
Stir for a minute, then garnish with a small twist of lemon.

The naming of food and drink is a culinary art form in its own right, and one that is best observed in bar culture. With food, a name is seldom more than descriptive, but with cocktails, a name has the opportunity to be truly evocative. Take "Treacle" for example: you might have never had one before, yet the name paints a vivid picture of something that is sweet, viscous and perhaps a little fruity. And that's exactly what a Treacle is.

The drink was invented by late, great British bartending legend Dick Bradsell, who was almost single-handedly responsible for the revival of cocktail culture in London during the late 1980s. Like most of Dick's drinks, Treacle is unpretentious and easy to put together. It's based on an Old Fashioned (Bourbon, sugar and bitters) but – given that this is a rum book – the whisky is replaced with pot-still rum, and a splash of apple juice is added to pep the whole thing up.

Dick was adamant that the drink should only be made with cheap (brown) apple juice, not the expensive pressed variety. And it's true that substituting one for the other does result in an entirely different kind of cocktail; both are tasty, but the cheap juice offers a glossier texture and a closer resemblance to treacle.

As for the rum, you're going to want something dense and funky to ride that apple wave. Jamaican is the obvious choice, but Demerara works equally well if it's genuine treacle flavour that you're after. Feeling experimental? Why not blend the two together? You can also experiment with switching up the sugar: for a darker variety, or for maple syrup, or honey.

SPICED RUMS

If there's one gaping omission from this book that will go unnoticed by some, it's that I have neglected to mention spiced or flavoured rums. Over half of the distilleries mentioned in this book produce a flavoured rum of one kind or another, and most of the blenders do too. In the UK, spiced/flavoured rum is the fastest growing category of rum style and in the past 10 years spiced rums have more than quadrupled in volume, and now constitute almost one-third of all the rum consumed in the British Isles! So why leave it out?

Well, for starters, they're not true rums. Spiced rums are flavoured and sweetened products that happen to be based on sugarcane, and most of them taste awful. Some, such as Morgan's Spiced, are not even legally classifiable as rum, because it falls under the minimum ABV requirement of 37.5% (study a bottle of Morgan Spiced and you'll notice that it never claims to be rum).

So instead of wasting pages of tasting notes that attempt to describe "vanilla" in all sorts of colourful language, I'm giving you, dear reader, a few recipes to make your own.

STEPHENSON'S SPICED

800 ML/27 FL. OZ. AGED BLENDED RUM

150 ML/5 FL. OZ. EXTRA-AGED POT-STILL RUM

10 G/⅓ FL. OZ. FRESH THYME LEAVES

5 G/⅛ OZ. CRUSHED ALLSPICE BERRIES

5 G /⅛ OZ. CRUSHED BLACK PEPPERCORNS

2 G /1⁄16 OZ. MACE BLADES • 1 G/1⁄32 OZ. GRATED NUTMEG

1 SMALL CINNAMON STICK • 3 STAR ANISE BLADES

2 G/1⁄16 OZ. SALT • 50 G/1⅔ OZ. SUGAR

50 ML/1⅔ FL. OZ. PEDRO XIMENEZ SHERRY

Add the rums and the spices and seasonings to a Kilner/Mason jar and allow to macerate for two weeks. Strain through muslin/cheesecloth, then sweeten the spirit with sherry and sugar to taste.

This is my recipe, but in theory you can use whatever spices you like, and if you don't like some of the ones that I've listed, by all means substitute them. One spice I would

avoid using at all costs, however, is vanilla. This is the most common ingredient you'll encounter in the spiced rum world, because it does an okay job of simulating

age in an un-aged rum base (which is what most spiced rum companies use). We have no need for a cover-up job, as it'll be good quality, aged rum that we're using in the first place. Adding vanilla will only serve to muddy the natural maturation distinction.

What we're looking to do with our spices is enhance the natural flavours of the rum and amplify the natural wood spices that you might encounter in a spirit aged in European oak casks. So think along the lines of clove, pimento, nutmeg, mace, ginger, cinnamon, pink peppercorn, cocoa and cardamom.

One approach to making spiced rum is to macerate each ingredient separately and then blend the infusions to the flavour that you desire. The only problem is, you might end up wasting some of your infusions if you only use a little.

PEPPERED PINEAPPLE

**500 G/18 OZ. WHITE CANE JUICE RUM
(PREFERABLY 55% ABV OR HIGHER)**

**400 G/14 OZ. PINEAPPLE, CUT INTO
CHUNKS, SKIN AND LEAVES INCLUDED**

10 G/⅓ OZ. PINK PEPPERCORNS

5G/⅛ OZ. GREEN CARDAMOM PODS

**400 ML/14 FL. OZ. AGED
POT-STILL RUM**

SUGAR (OPTIONAL)

Mix the white rum with the pineapple
chunks and spices and allow to sit for two
weeks. Carefully pour off the rum (which
will float), strain the liquid through muslin/
cheesecloth, then mix with the pot-still
rum to finish.

The best flavoured rum on the market is
without doubt Plantation Pineapple (see
pages 89–91). It is a tribute to the esteemed
Reverend Stiggins whose favourite drink
was the "pineapple rum" in *The Pickwick
Papers* by Charles Dickens. According to
booze historian David Wondrich, Dickens's
cellar was also known to keep a stock of
"fine old pine-apple rum". The production
process of Plantation's rum is complex, as
different parts of the pineapple are distilled
or macerated with Plantation rums, before
being separately aged and blended together
to form the finished product. The effort is
worth it, though, and evident in the
authentic, not-too-sweet but not-too-dry,
green pineapple taste coupled with actual
rum flavour.

My Peppered Pineapple is far easier to
put together, and still produces results that
are better than most spiced rums. The
sweetness of the finished product will vary
depending on how ripe your pineapple is.

PIMENTO DRAM

**500 ML/17 FL. OZ. OVERPROOF
JAMAICAN RUM**

**100 G/7 OZ. CRUSHED (OR BLENDED)
PIMENTO BERRIES**

1 SMALL CINNAMON STICK

15 G/⅛ OZ. WHOLE MACE BLADES

**500 ML/17 FL. OZ. AGED
POT-STILL RUM**

**600 G/21 OZ. CASTER/SUPERFINE
SUGAR**

300 ML/10½ FL. OZ. WATER

Add the spices and overproof rum to a
kilner jar and allow to infuse for a couple
of weeks. The high-strength spirit acts as
a better solvent than a lower-strength
spirit, so extracts flavour more effectively.
Strain the spices out and mix the infusion
with the pot-still rum. In a pan, gently heat
the sugar and water until the sugar
dissolves. Mix the syrup with your
spice infusion and bottle.

Pimento dram is a traditional liqueur
in Jamaica, which is made using the
trademark flavour of pimento/allspice
berries. Ten years ago, this stuff was hard
to find outside of Jamaica, but there are a
couple of off-the-shelf options available
these days (St. Elizabeth and Bitter Truth,
for example), which can be put to good
use in a whole variety of cocktails such
as sours and swizzles.

In effect this is a much sweeter,
single-spice version of spiced rum. I've
added cinnamon and mace to mine too,
which are not supposed to be detectable
in the flavour of liqueur, but rather bolster
some of the more subtle facets of the
allspice zing.

FALERNUM

400 ML/14 FL. OZ. WHITE BLENDED RUM

30 G/1 OZ. CHOPPED APRICOTS

10 G/⅓ OZ. KAFFIR LIME LEAVES

5 G/⅛ OZ. CHOPPED LEMONGRASS

3 G/¹⁄₁₆ OZ. GROUND GINGER

2 G/¹⁄₁₆ OZ. CLOVES

300 G/10½ OZ. SUGAR

400 ML/14 FL. OZ. WATER

5 G/⅛ OZ. CITRIC ACID

5 G /⅛ OZ. SALT

3 G/¹⁄₁₆ OZ. ASCORBIC ACID

Add the fruit and spices to the rum and allow to infuse in a Kilner/Mason jar for at least a week. Strain, then mix the other ingredients in until the sugar has dissolved.

You're not a Tiki bar unless you have a good stock of falernum – it's called for in all manner of Tiki drinks. The ingredient seems to have originated in Barbados where it is based on a mixture of rum, ginger, almond, cloves, and most important of all, lime. As for when it was invented, nobody seems to have a conclusive answer. One of the earliest written references comes from an 1892 edition of Victorian magazine *All Year Round*, which talks of "a curious liqueur composed of rum and lime juice."

Taylor's Velvet Falernum is the best-known brand of falernum, and was developed by John D. Taylor in Bridgetown, Barbados. These days it's made at the Foursquare distillery.

My recipe calls for lime leaves and lemongrass in place of the fruit, as the flavour is more aromatic and more consistent. I add a touch of citric and ascorbic acid to emulate the subtle acidity of a classic falernum. The apricots are unconventional, but they add some almond aroma and also give the liquid some body and colour.

RUM AND RAISIN ICE-CREAM

100 G/3½ OZ. EGG YOLKS

5 G/⅛ OZ. SOYA LECITHIN (FOR CREAMINESS)

75 G/2⅔ OZ. SUGAR

150 ML/5 FL. OZ. AGED POT-STILL RUM

75 ML/2.5 FL. OZ. PEDRO XIMENEZ WINE

40 G/1½ OZ. MILK POWDER

300 ML/10 FL. OZ. WHOLE MILK

50 ML/1⅔ FL. OZ. DOUBLE/HEAVY CREAM

Add each ingredient to a stainless-steel food mixer on a medium speed in the order listed above, leaving the first three to mix on their own at high-speed for a couple of minutes. Once everything is in there and mixed to a smooth batter, add sufficient liquid nitrogen to freeze the ice cream into a solid, creamy mass. In the unlikely event that you don't have any liquid nitrogen handy, this recipe can be made in a household ice-cream maker.

Imagine my surprise when I discovered – after creating a rum and sultana/golden raisin flavoured cocktail – that there was once a place called the Sultanate of Rûm. Bearing absolutely no connection to rum the drink (or dried grapes for that matter), the Sultanate of Rûm was a Muslim state that existed between Turkey and Persia during the Middle Ages. Now, with that brief history lesson behind us, let's get on with discovering more about this boozy dessert.

One of my favourite childhood treats was rum and raisin ice-cream – in fact it's probably where I first encountered the taste of rum. That sensation of the raisins popping in your mouth, while the sweet and silky rum flavoured ice-cream cools your palate. It seems like an obvious pairing of flavours, and when you consider the intense, heady, bordering-on-boozy sweetness of dried fruit, it's no great wonder that spirits pair so well with it. And with the possible exception of brandy, there's no better example than rum, where oak and spice reformulate the DNA of the fruit, amplifying and embellishing the natural flavours.

Dried fruit and alcohol has a much longer history than ice-cream, as folks have been using wine to preserve fruits since Ancient Egyptian times. Later, these preserved fruits were used as ingredients in baking, to make steamed puddings, fruit cakes, flans, and that queen of British desserts – trifle.

In the context of ice-cream, rum and raisins first encountered each other in Italy, where the combination is often referred to as "Málaga". This name comes from the specific variety of Málaga raisins that are used in the preparation, which are made from Muscat and Alexandria grape varieties – both known for their high natural sugar content. The Sicilians were the first ones to create Málaga gelato, which was originally made with sweet wine instead of rum. The raisins were soaked overnight and mixed into vanilla gelato, providing a sweet burst of alcohol in every bite. The trend caught on, and in the 1980s, Häagen-Dazs introduced a rum and raisin ice cream to the US market.

My ice-cream recipe doesn't use raisins as such, but instead calls for Pedro Ximenez wine. This dessert wine, is like bottled concentrated sultana (golden raisin) flavour. It's technically a sherry, matured in oak casks in Spain – some of which are used to mature rums. The wine takes on a thick, glossy lustre, and it positively turbo-charges the flavour of my ice cream. The rest of the ingredients are quite standard. I chose to use a combination of Jamaican pot-still and Demerara rums, which nudges that high-ester flavour right to the forefront of the dessert.

You can make this drink using an ice-cream maker, but for best results, I recommend using dry-ice or liquid nitrogen – both of which are surprisingly easy to track down these days.

DIRECTORY OF DISTILLERIES

This appendix recognizes both the big and small brands, and it will hopefully give you an introduction into the depth and breadth of rum-making going on around the world today. Do bear in mind that this list is by no means exhaustive.

ANTIGUA

The Antigua Distillery Limited

Situated on a peninsula in St. John's, the ADL was set up in 1932 by three Portuguese rum vendors. The highlight of this distillery is the all-copper-everything triple column still. Due to the risk of tropical storms, it has been chopped up to lower the height, which means that there are in fact five columns that operate as if they are three. Their English Harbour rum has won awards for its complex maturation characteristics.

ARGENTINA

Pablo Ibarreche

Located in Tucumán, the sugarcane-growing region of Argentina, this copper column distillery produces a white rum from a long (one-week) fermentation of molasses. The rum made here is branded as "Isla Ñ" and includes a gold rum matured in French oak casks.

AUSTRALIA

Beenleigh

This longstanding distillery is based on an old mill established by English farmers John Davy and Francis Gooding, near Brisbane in the 1880s. They produce rum in a similar fashion to bourbon whiskey, by first stripping fermented molasses in a wash column, then increasing its strength in an old copper pot still that's aptly named "Old Copper". They bottle a white rum, a 5-year-old and a no-age statement rum.

Bundaberg

The iconic Queensland distillery often referred to as "Bundy" started life as a sugar mill before the Bundaberg Distilling Company began operations in 1888. The bottle's label depicts a polar bear, thought to imply the warming qualities of the rum. These days it's owned by Diageo and produces numerous expressions including Red and Master Distiller's Collection.

Hoochery

Claiming to make the only rum produced in Western Australia, Hoochery is a farm distillery in Kununurra which produces about 50,000 bottles of Ord River rum a year. The products are made from local cane, fermented, distilled and bottled on-site. As the owner, Raymond (Spike) Dessert III, says, "there are no gimmicks and no fancy label, just bloody good dinky-di Kimberley Spirit to enjoy around the table!"

Mt. Uncle

As the name implies, this distillery is set high up in the Cairns highlands. The cane for their rum is sourced locally, and its syrup is used to make their 37% ABV Platinum Cane Spirit. Mt. Uncle also produce Iridium Gold Rum which is matured for four years in oak casks.

BARBADOS

Foursquare

The roots of this distillery can be traced back to Reginald Leon Seale, who began blending and selling rum in 1926, before passing the business down through four family generations. They built the state-of-the-art Foursquare Distillery in the 1990s on the site of the old Foursquare mill and began distilling their own

LEFT The visitors' centre at Foursquare, Barbados, is a must-see. Foursquare produce everything, from £8 ($10) bottles of Old Brigand, to single pot-still rums that fetch hundreds of dollars at auction.

BELOW LEFT Mount Gay Black Barrel: while harder to track down, this rum contains a high proportion of pot-still spirit compared to "Eclipse" and it is finished in heavily charred ex-bourbon barrels.

Aubrey Ward and business partner John Hutson took over and brought Mount Gay to the international market. Rémy Cointreau bought a large shareholding in 1989. Well known blends include Eclipse, Mount Gay XO and the more elusive Black Barrel.

St. Nicholas Abbey

In 2006, the cane plantation and old abbey (which has no religious connection) were purchased by architect Larry Warren, who beautifully restored the building. Bottling of rum started in 2009 and distilling in 2013. Production is managed by Larry's son, Simon, who has installed sustainable practices like using the leftover *bagasse* from their cane to power the steam boiler. A white rum and a 5-year-old are made on site, but some of the older expressions were actually made at Foursquare distillery.

The West Indies Rum Distillery

Barbados's biggest distillery produces the tropical tasting Malibu coconut liqueur for Pernod Ricard, as well as the Cockspur brand. It was built in 1893 by George and Herman Stade, who introduced the first column still to Barbados. The distillery was nationalized and became The West India Rum Refinery in 1918. It was bought by the Goddard family in 1973. Column stills are used to make Malibu but, true to Barbadian style, a mixture of pot and column made spirits are blended for the Cockspur.

expressions, all of which contain a pot-still component. Now run by master distiller Richard Seale, Foursquare also produce Barbadian brands including R. L. Seale's Finest Rum, Doorly's Macaw and Old Brigand.

Mount Gay

One of the oldest rum distilleries in the world, William Sandiford established the "Mount Gilboa" site in the early 18th century. The Sober family bought the distillery in 1747 and asked their friend Sir John Gay Alleyne to manage it. In 1852 it was renamed Mount Gay in Sir John's honour. In the early 20th century,

BELIZE
Cuello
This Belizean distillery was founded by Ignacio Cuello in the 1950s. It's still family-operated and produces the top-selling domestic rum in Belize. Exports are finding their way into the US.

Travellers Liquors Ltd.
With its origins in a bar in Belize City, Travellers became a rum blender, and then distillery in the 1960s. After 50-or-so years, it's still operated by the Perdomo family, who bottle under the Belizean Rum brand name among others.

BRAZIL
Oronoco
A rum distilled by cachaça makers Vicente and Roberto Bastos Ribeiro. Oronoco gets 10/10 for its leather bound packaging embossed with a map of Brazil. The rum is based on fermented cane juice, triple-distilled in copper columns, then blended with un-aged Venezuelan rum, before being finished in Brazilian Amendoim casks and then filtered to remove colour.

BRITISH VIRGIN ISLANDS
Callwood Distillery
This distillery on Tortola was acquired by the Callwood family in the late 1800s and is run by their descendants today. Methods and equipment have not changed much, and the staff here perform their roles like caretakers to tradition, seemingly unaware of the finer details of their process. The rum is tasty though, thanks to a long fermentation and low-strength distillation. They make a white rum, 4-year-old, 10-year-old and a rum liqueur called "The Panty Dropper".

CAYMAN ISLANDS
Seven Fathoms
Founded by Walker Romanica and Nelson Dilbert in 2007, this distillery relocated to George Town in 2013. According to Cayman Spirits Co., Seven Fathoms rum is a blend of one-, two- and three-year-old rums, all of which have spent time maturing under the sea. This may sound like a logistical nightmare, but the family of one of the proprietors owns a diving company, so they have the equipment they need.

CUBA
Havana Club
This iconic brand paints a romantic picture of jazz, mojitos and cigars. José Arechabala first registered Havana Club in 1934, before his distillery was seized by Castro in 1960. Castro then teamed up with Pernod Ricard to begin producing his own Havana Club, while the Arechabala family responded by pairing with Bacardí to make their own

ABOVE Havana Club Añejo 3 Años: one of the true icons of the rum world.

in America. Lawsuits followed. Both versions now co-exist, though most of the world drinks Pernod Ricard's Cuban version. Apart from premium expressions, most Havana Club rums are ideal for mixing.

Tecnoazucar

This rum powerhouse was founded by Heriberto Duquesne in the 1960s, and is located in the central region of Cuba at Villa Clara. The distillery produces rum for a whole range of Cuban brands, most notably Ron Mulata, and Ron Vigia, the former being a rum that is beginning to gather pace internationally.

DOMINICA
Shillingford

Howell Donald Shillingford bought the Macoucherie Estate in 1942 and started producing cane juice rum. Today the business is run by Don Shillingford who oversaw its rehabilitation after Hurricane Erica in 2015. He plans to release more premium aged expressions alongside their unaged and overproof varieties.

DOMINICAN REPUBLIC
Barceló

First established in 1930 by Julián Barceló, the brand has since been bought by Spanish investors and merged with

Varma International, prompting huge export trade. Their Añejo and Gran Añejo expressions are blends of 2- and 3-year-old, and 4- and 6-year old rums respectively. Gran Platinum is a 6-year-old clear filtered rum and the brand's flagship, Imperial, comprises 8–10-year old rums. Flashy offerings include the Imperial Onyx, which is filtered through Mexican onyx stones.

Brugal

Founder Andrés Brugal Montaner went into business in 1888 and became known as a great rum blender. Edrington Group bought a majority in 2008, but operations remain in the hands of Brugal's fifth generation. Brugal employ three distilleries to produce their spirit, which by their own admission gets its character from ex-bourbon and sherry casks. The top-level oak comes into its own in the older expressions, where wood spice, dried fruits and sweet dairy notes win me over. The 1888 variety is my pick.

FIJI
South Pacific Distilleries

Based on the island of Lautoka, this distillery produces spirit for the Fiji Rum Co., who bottle Bounty Rum as well as supplying rums to various independent bottlers including Duncan

Taylor, Hunter Laing and Cadenhead. The rums are based on Fijian sugar derived molasses.

GRENADA
Grenada Sugar Factory
The factory and distillery were built in 1937 by a collective of sugar planters. Their best-known brand, Clarke's Court, was created in 1973, though it would have been different to the ones made today. The ability of this operation to adapt through political revolution, privatization and raw material changes is what's kept it alive, but today they use imported molasses and some character of spirit has been lost.

River Antoine Distillery
Established in 1785, the rum made here is strong stuff, but the observation of historical methods is stronger still. The distillery is powered by a water wheel, which helps process the locally supplied hand-cut cane into juice. No yeast is added, instead natural airborne yeast, Grenadian sunshine and a cocktail of bacteria in the tanks are relied on to ferment the liquid, which is made into rum in copper pot stills heated by a wood burning furnace. I pray it never changes.

GUADELOUPE
Bellevue
The Damoiseau family bought the old distillery with its iconic windmill in 1924 and it has been with them ever since. In 1995, they merged with La Martiniquase, which channelled investment into creating a sustainable business and they are now a carbon negative operation. Around 95% of the produced here is bottled as "*rhum blanc*" (unaged cane juice rum), the remaining 5% is matured in ex-bourbon and ex-Cognac casks.

Bielle
This progressive distillery is based in Marie-Galante and run by manager Jérôme Thiery and cellar master Jacques Larrent. Their artfully made Bielle branded cane juice *rhums* are column still produced, then cut to strength with

BELOW Both of River Antoine's products are twice the strength and half the price of Bacardi.

BOTTOM 59% ABV Marie-Galante packs some heat.

rainwater. The award winning Rhum Rhum brand has been made here since 2007 in partnership with Gianni Capovilla and Luca Gargano. The undiluted cane juice has a long fermentation before being twice-distilled in a copper pot still. The pot is also used to re-distil Bielle's Premium Blanc *rhum agricole* – one of the best.

Distillerie Bologne

On the edge of Basse-Terre is Distillerie Bologne, a fortress of an operation. Originally owned by the Bolognes family, the estate changed hands before being bought by the Sargenton-Callard family in 1930, who still own it today. *Rhum Bologne* is distilled to 55–60% ABV, which means less of the cane juice flavour is lost. Older expressions are aged in French oak Cognac and Armagnac casks. Releases, such as the VSOP (Very Superior Old Pale) are unmatched on this, or any island, perhaps.

Domaine de Damoiseau

Guadeloupe's largest distillery is located in the Grande-Terre countryside. Roger Damoiseau bought it back in 1942 and made it a great success. The current owner is Hervé Damoiseau, a man with a passionate and eccentric approach. As well as some aged varieties, they produce perhaps the lightest of any French *rhum agricole* distillates thanks to the 12-plate Coffey still, which pumps out white *rhum* at 88% ABV.

Domaine de Sevérin

This distillery occupies the north of Basse-Terre. Monsieur Sevérin bought the estate in the 19th century before it was acquired by Ms. Beauvarlet in 1920,

who put her nephew, Henri Marsolle, in charge. His grandsons later took over and in 2014 a majority was sold to José Pirbakas. Hand-cut cane is juiced and fermented here for 48 hours before being single column distilled. The result is an angry little spirit, but Sevérin's aged expression tempers some of that aggression.

Longueteau

Set up in 1895 by Henri Longueteau, this Basse-Terre based distillery has been run by the same family since. They grow their own supply of cane here, the fermented juice of which is sent to a stainless-steel column still. The white Longueteau *rhum* is rested for three months, giving it a nice edge. The Karukera brand's *rhum agricole*, made only with blue cane and naturally fermented, is also produced here. The

GUATEMALA
Industrias Licoreras de Guatemala

Established by the Botran brothers in the early 20th century, the Botran and Zacapa brands are produced here, both of which are marketed as super-premium. Both are distilled from fermented virgin sugarcane honey and are made using a "solera" system, which involves blending rums of four cask types with measures of older stocks from previous blends. Look out for the Reserva and Solera 1893 expressions.

GUYANA
Diamond Distillery

The massive still house of this incredible operation contains 14 pieces of apparatus that produce over two dozen styles of molasses-based rum. They use everything from copper pot stills to French Savalle four-column stills, but by far the most famous pieces of kit are the world's only functioning wooden stills (three pot and one column). These historic artefacts create the unique spirits crucial to the El Dorado blends, a brand also renowned for its sweetness.

HAITI
Arawaks

Located in Cavaillon, the diesel-fuelled mill of this distillery processes the cane juice, which is then naturally fermented for 1–2 weeks. It's distilled in a pot still resembling a large domed trash can. Arawaks clairin is then bottled by the rum company Velier under the Clairin Vaval brand name. The operation is run by Fritz Vaval, an ambitious man who is testing fruit-flavoured clairins and aging in charred oak casks.

aged varieties of both these *rhums* steal the show after being matured in French oak casks.

Montebello

Formerly known as the Carrère Distillery, Montebello is based in the town of Petit-Bourg. It was established in 1930 by the Dolomite family, then sold to the Marsolle family in 1968 who run it today. It's a mechanical wonder to behold, with a tangle of corrugated iron and pipes. Casks of the column copper distilled *rhum agricole* are kept in sheet metal warehouses, effectively baking in the sunshine.

Poisson

Built in 1916 on the west coast of Marie-Galante, this distillery make the popular Père Labat brand of *rhum*. Production processes fit the standard agricole mould, but the equipment is old and battered. Quality varies, but the 18- year-old Cuvée 1997 is a diamond in the rough.

Barbancourt

Much national pride surrounds Haiti's only internationally recognized *rhum* brand. It was set up in 1862 by Dupré Barbancourt and passed to the hands of the Gardère family. The distillery can be found in Port-au-Prince and is a fiercely self-sufficient operation. The production here is similar to other *agricole* distilleries, but when it gets to the virgin Limousin oak casks, the spirit is mixed with spices to make up for the loss of characteristics during distillation.

Chelo

This small distillery belonging to Michel Sajous is located in the town of Saint Michel de l'Attalaye in the *Massif du Nord* mountains. Chelo make their clairin from fermented sugarcane syrup in a pot still.

INDIA
Mohan Meakin

Based in Uttar Pradesh, this Indian producer makes the cult brand Old Monk. The product has been around since the 1950s and has grown to become one of the best-selling rum brands in the world (though it's rarely seen outside of India). The popular "Dark" expression is blended from a selection of rums, which are (allegedly) aged for a minimum of eight years.

United Spirits

Producer of the world's biggest selling rum brand – Mc Dowell's No.1 Celebration – which was first introduced in 1991. It's not exported, and little is known about the production specifics, but they sure sell a lot of it.

JAMAICA
Appleton Estate

Appleton is the international ambassador for Jamaican rum. The estate grows the 10 varieties of cane used to produce its own rums and master blender, Joy Spence, claims the superior terroir is what gives them their orange peel top note. Dating back to 1749, Appleton was originally owned by the Dickinson family and bought by J. Wray & Nephew in 1916. (Wray & Nephew rum itself being one the most popular brands in Jamaica and produced at Appleton's sister distillery, New Yarmouth) The Campari Group bought J. Wray & Nephew in 2012.

Clarendon

Jamaica's biggest rum-maker, located near the south coast, is owned by Diageo, DDL of Guyana, Goddard Enterprises and the Jamaican government. A fraction of the spirit made here goes into small Jamaican brands or bottles of Monymusk Overproof, which was launched in 2011 but is rarely seen. The rest is bottled by

BELOW Wray & Nephew is the most popular rum brand in Jamaica, and it's produced at Appleton's sister distillery, New Yarmouth.

Diageo in their Captain Morgan rum sold in Europe and in their legendary Myer's brand. Around three-quarters of the fermented molasses here is distilled in a cutting-edge column still and the rest in one of two pot stills.

Hampden

Hampden estate was founded in 1756 by Archibald Sterling. After changing hands, it was bought by the Hussey family in 2009. The brand is the champion of higher ester rum, thanks to an intense fermentation promoted by the use of dunder and years of microbiological activity in the vats. Hampden's strongest ester rum is used as flavouring in confectionery, but do try their high ester DOK high overproof rum, or sample it blended in a bottle of Smith and Cross.

Worthy Park

The Clarke family bought the Worthy Park sugar plant in 1918 and built the smart new distillery in 2007. Molasses is fermented in three different ways to create various ester strengths, then distilled in a Forsyths pot still. Around a third of the spirit is sold to third parties including Bacardí for their Single Cane Estate range and popular "The Duppy

BELOW Green cane at dusk at the Hampden Estate. No other island identifies with rum and sugar at such a fundamental level as Jamaica and the Jamaicans.

Share" blend. Half appears in Worthy Park's own Rum Bar label and the rest is kept in casks for a rainy day.

JAPAN

Nine Leaves

Based in the Shiga Prefecture, Nine Leaves produce the better of the available Japanese rums in my opinion. The base is Japanese muscovado sugar, and spirit is distilled in copper pots. They bottle Clear, Almost Spring, which is aged for six months in Cabernet Sauvignon casks; and two Angel's Half releases, each matured in American or French oak for six months.

Kiksui

This distillery produces an expensive rum from sugarcane grown on the island of Shikoku, which they age in oak barrels for seven years and bottle under the Ryoma label. The rum is light and vegetal, smelling of Marmite and tar.

MARTINIQUE

Depaz

Set on Mount Pelée volcano, Depaz distillery was established in 1917 by Victor Depaz, 15 years after it erupted and killed his family. The story ends happier in that he was very successful, and Depaz is now owned by La Martiniquaise. Stainless-steel stills are used to distil Depaz *rhums*, producing a

ABOVE Trois Rivières is one of the better-known Martinican export brands, even though the distillery closed 15 years ago.

selection of *blanc* and *vieux* that speak of the Caribbean sea. Dillon *rhums* are also produced here in a copper still.

J.M

Jean-Marie Martin founded J.M near Mount Pelée in 1845 among thriving cane and banana plantations; it managed to survive the 1902 blast. Now owned by the Bernard Hayot Group, quality is the priority and workers aim to mill the cane within an hour of cutting it. The *rhum agricole* is distilled through a copper column and finished with volcanic spring water. The *rhum blanc* is rested in steel for six months and the rest sent to a humid barrel house.

La Favorite

This humble little distillery is the last remaining in Fort-de-France. It's the longest continuously family-run

distillery on Martinique, having been in the Domoy family for three generations. They make a small range of no-frills *rhums* and an even smaller range of *vieux* expressions.

La Mauny

The estate was bought by the Bellonie brothers in 1923, who began creating *rhum agricole*. In 1994, La Mauny acquired the Trois Rivières and Duquesne rum brands, and the whole lot is now owned by the Chevrillon Group. The enormous crane grabber that collects the cane to send to a sophisticated computerised mill system indicates the scale of the operation here, as does the aircraft hangar of a still house with five column stills. There are 27 fermentation vats and six different yeast strains. Most of the casks that house the white rum are ex-bourbon or French.

Le Simon

Instead of producing under its own name, Le Simon is surrogate parent to Clément and Habitation Saint-Étienne (HSE) *rhum agricoles* and some other smaller labels. Both these larger brands

BELOW The Clément range covers a rainbow of colours and all manner of flavours (except rainbow flavour).

are transported away for ageing, blending and bottling. Some of the most sought-after rums in the Caribbean have been, and still are, bottled under the Clément name and HSE is available in an impressive array of marques, from standard white to extra-aged and liquids finished in single malt, sherry and Sauterne casks.

Neisson
It may be the smallest distillery on Martinique, but Neisson's white *rhum* is the most popular on the island. Located in Le Carbet, production began in 1931 and the distillery is still family run today. They achieve complexly flavoured rums with a proprietary yeast strain and a long fermentation. Distillation takes place in a copper Savalle still and aged varieties are matured for at least four years in ex-bourbon or French oak casks. Neisson have also created a range of white *rhums* that each use different varieties of cane, one of which is boldly bottled at 70% ABV.

Saint James
Martinique's largest *rhum agricole* distillery has survived through the volcanic decimation of its original site and bankruptcy at the existing site in

Sainte-Marie. Today the business is run by La Martiniquaise group. Jean Claude Benoît has managed things since the 1980s, preserving the artisanal practices through expansion. A huge range is produced here, including many aged *rhums* with double-digit maturation periods.

MAURITIUS
Charamel
Producer of a great range of *agricole* rums made from cane grown on their own estate. Charamel use both a copper column and pair of copper pots to make two distinct distillates for their range of expressions. The products feel quite Cognac-esque in their styling and naming convention. The Single Barrel 2008 is a belter.

Grays & Co.
This company started out as an investment firm that bought the "OK Distillery" in the 1930s. They diversified into spirits in the 1980s and renamed Gran's Refinery. They produce rum under the New Grove brand, which traverses a broad section of styles with half a dozen bottles. Featuring both molasses and cane juice bases, there's everything from un-aged agricole, to a 25-year-old solera in a crystal decanter.

Medine
The Medine Sugar Factory and Distillery has been in continuous operation since 1926 and it forms one half of the Penny Blue Rum partnerships with Berry Bros. & Rudd.

Oxenham
Edward Clark Oxenham founded his

LEFT Martinique's biggest distillery is just like the Saint James bottle: square-shaped and full of rhum.

wine import business in 1932, and in the 1980s, the company branched out into spirits. They now produce and bottle Fregate Rum which is column-distilled from molasses.

Rhumerie des Mascareignes
This distillery was built in 2006 as part of a huge renovation project on the 150-year-old Château de Labourdonnais. The distillery uses a column still to produce pure two labels of *agricole* rum: Rhumeur and La Bourdonnais.

St. Aubin
A Mauritius-based distillery producing rums in the *agricole* fashion from sugarcane juice. Along with *blanc* and *vieux* expressions, St. Aubin also bottle various flavoured rums. You can spot St. Aubin thanks to its squat, square-shaped bottle.

THE NETHERLANDS
Zuidam
The Zuidam family have been distilling in the Dutch village of Baarle-Nassau for 40 years, and along with the production of genever, gin and whisky, they also make "the first rum distilled in mainland Europe" under the Flying Dutchman brand name. It's distilled from a molasses base, in copper pot stills, and matured for 12 months (No. 1) or 36 months (No. 3) – the latter seeing some time in oloroso and PX casks, too.

NICARAGUA
Flor de Caña
The distilling company Compañia Licorera de Nicaragua (CLN) dates back to 1937 and Flor de Caña was born in 1996 after a distillery upgrade. Innovative energy saving practices here include the collecting of carbon dioxide from fermentation, which is sold to the

ABOVE Flor de Caña rums are entirely column-distilled, which means almost all of the flavour comes from the barrel. Fortunately, the cellar masters Compañia Locker de Nicaragua seem to know what they are doing, as Flor de Caña 7 is a cracking rum for the price.

Coca-Cola bottling plant. Each expression is distilled to a unique specification using a combination of columns in the still. Almost all of the flavour comes from the barrel, but that seems to work well for these award-winning rums.

PANAMA
Las Cabras
La Cabras was established in the 1990s by legendary distiller and Cuban national Franciso Jose "Don Pancho" Fernandez Perez. He took over a defunct mill in the Las Cabras region and restored the languishing four-column copper still which makes all the rums there today.

Don Pancho produces for brands such as Cana Brava and Selvarey rum. He has developed his own proprietary yeast strain for his range of Cuban style "Don Pancho Origines" rums, which are available in 8-, 18- and 30-year-old expressions.

Varela Hermanos

Don José Varela Blanco founded this distillery in Pesé, now in its third generation of family ownership. Here they produce the nation's favourite drink, Seco Herrerano, but outside of Panama are better known for their classifiable rums – the cane honey based Ron Abuelo and the molasses based Cortez. Each base is fermented using a proprietary yeast strain before passing through a four column still. Expressions include an "Anjeo" plus 7-, 12- and 15-year-old (XV), the latter in a variety of cask finishes.

PARAGUAY
Hogerzeil

Located just outside of Asunción, this distillery produces both molasses rum and a pot-still *rhum agricole* bottled under the Jules Verne label. There's no added sugar or caramel here, and to top it all off, their cane is certified organic!

Papagayo

This Paraguayan distillery was founded in 1993 by Eduardo Felippo and a co-operative for local sugarcane smallholders. It has since expanded to incorporate some 1,000 families. The rum made here is based on molasses, available in White and Golden expressions, and produced in a pot-still juice. It's certified organic and Fair Trade.

PERÚ
Cartavio

Founded in 1929, Cartavio have been knocking out some decent bottles under their own brand and as wholesale rums to third parties. The distillery features a stainless-steel column still and copper pot, and their cellars house American, French and Slovenian oak casks.

PHILIPPINES
Tanduay

The Tanduay Distillery in Manilla was founded in 1854. They produce one of the best-selling rum brands in the world – Tanduay. Despite these being a mix of industrial alcohol, sugar and other flavours, they taste better than you might expect, especially the 12-year-old Superior.

PUERTO RICO
Bacardí

This family-owned empire operates three distilleries in Puerto Rico, Mexico and India. There are none in its native Cuba, following the seizure of assets there by Castro in 1960. Don Facundo Bacardí Massó founded the brand with José Léon Boutellier in Santiago in 1862. They established the winning formula brand in the world. Stocks of the precious old yeast strain are today still used to ferment the molasses. The low-strength *aguardiente* and high-strength *redistillaro* are each made in a column still, then matured and charcoal-filtered before blending. Famous expressions include Carta Blanca, Carta Oro (gold), Black, Bacardí Carta, Ocho 8 Años and the fantastic Casa Bacardí Special Reserve.

Club Caribe
Opened in 2012, Club Caribe is based in the mountain town of Cidra. It's an arm of Florida Caribbean Distillers, who own two further distilleries in Florida. For tax break purposes, molasses is fermented and distilled through a five column set

BELOW The bat symbol is said to have derived from the family of bats that lived in the rafters of the original distillery.

up in Florida, then transported to Club Caribe to be distilled for a final time.

Cruz
A small distillery built in 2009 near the town of Juyuya. They bottle two white rums: the stronger PitoRico 106, designed to be a legal portrayal of traditional *pitorro* (Puerto Rican moonshine) and PitoRico Elite, a softer un-aged white rum.

Serrallés
Located in the city of Ponce, this distillery was founded by Juan Serrallés in 1861 and is now in its sixth generation of family ownership. As well as producing Don Q, the island's best-selling rum, Serrallés have acquired the Puerto Rico Distillers, Inc, the licence to manufacture Captain Morgan and many local brands. The range of Don Q rums includes a white 12-month aged Cristal, Don Q Añejo, Gran Añejo and Gran Reserva de la Familia – a blend of rums at least 20-years-old.

RÉUNION
Isautier
Réunion's oldest distillery was founded in 1845 and has been in the hands of the Isautier family ever since. In 2011, the distillery moved from its original location to a modern production plant. They make *traditionnel* and *agricole* rums, as well as *vieux* expressions matured in French oak.

Rivière du Mât
Producer of molasses and cane juice rums from Réunion cane. This distillery specializes in older rums, such as their Agricole Reserve 6-year-old and those from 2004 and beyond.

Savanna

A producer of both cane juice and *agricole* rums, Savanna was founded in 1948. My pick of their range is their 5-year-old molasses-based Grand Arôme, which is finished in port barrels.

ST LUCIA
St Lucia Distillers

In 1972 the Barnard family joined with Geest industries and moved their operation to the Roseau Valley, forming St Lucia Distillers. They spent time recovering from an arson attack in 2007, but today represent the best of Caribbean rum which is made in their collection of copper pot and column stills. Releases such as Chairman's Reserve and Admiral Rodney have been a hit in the premium export market. The Bernard Hayot Group purchased them in 2016.

ABOVE Blending column and pot-still rums is a sure bet when it comes to producing characterful spirit. Both of these products are made in that fashion at St. Lucia Distillers, though Elements 8 is a privately owned brand.

ST VINCENT AND THE GRENADINES
St Vincent Distillers

The current private owners bought this Georgetown distillery in 1996. Their molasses is imported from Guyana, but the distillery takes water from the Georgetown River for finishing its column still made rum. Their Captain Bligh XO won World's Best Golden Rum and World's Best Rum at the World Drink Awards in 2014 and their Sunset Very Strong Rum won the World's Best Overproof Rum award in 2016.

SOUTH AFRICA
Mainstay

The legendary South African "Cane" was released in 1954 and sold in local shebeens. From the 1960s, consumers got a taste for cane spirits, and Mainstay became the top-selling brand in the country. It's five-column distilled and almost tastes like vodka.

TAHITI
Mana'o

Translating to "thought" or "desire" this Tahitian rum is made in the *agricole* style, from cane grown on the island of Taha'a. The cane is pressed and fermented, then sent by schooner to Paea, where it's distilled in a copper pot by the liquor firm Avatea and bottled as a white rum.

TRINIDAD AND TOBAGO
Angostura

Angostura rums only account for 3% of production at this vast high-tech distillery near Port of Spain. The rest is made up of local brands, wholesale rum for independent blenders and the rum used as a base for producing this distillery's best-known product: Angostura Bitters. All the rum made here is molasses-based and column distilled. They have one of

the largest holding stocks of maturing rum anywhere in the world, all in ex-bourbon casks.

Caroni
This Trinidad distillery was founded in 1923 but closed by Angostura (who at the time held 49% of the company's shares) in 2002. The distillery was renowned for a much heavier style of rum than Angostura, though it was also made in a column still. Caroni bottlings are still being released by the likes of Velier and Rum Nation.

UK
Matugga
A Cambridgeshire distillery making rum from African molasses in a 200-litre (53-US gallon) pot still. Matugga Golden Rum is matured for an undisclosed period in English oak casks and bottled at 42% ABV.

Spirit Masters
Cambridge-based distillers of Glorious Revolution! Rum which launched in 2014. The products made from fermented molasses are sourced from Africa and the Americas, and distilled on a tiny copper pot still.

USA
Canon Beach
An Oregon-based distillery that uses cane syrup as the base material for its Dorymen's Rum, their un-aged expression, and molasses for its Donlon Shanks Amber rum. Both are distilled on a custom-made Vendome rectifier.

Haleakala Distillers
Located on the slopes of Haleakala volcano, Maui, this distillery was founded in 2003 by Jim Sargent and is the first Hawaiian distillery since the 1970s. They make Maui Gold rum, but it's difficult to get hold of outside of Hawaii.

Journeyman
Based in Michigan, this distillery produces whiskey as well as Road's End Rum, which is made from organic molasses and matured in Featherbone Bourbon barrels for 12 months.

Lost Spirits
A California-based distillery and bottler specializing in "flash-ageing", which uses photocatalytic light to break down wood polymers and dramatically speed up the maturation process (so they say). The reactor can mimic a maturation of up to 20 years in just 6–8 days. Lost Spirits currently bottle a 68% Navy Rum, and Cuban inspired aged overproof.

Louisiana Spirits
Bayou branded rums are pot-distilled from unrefined Louisiana cane sugar and molasses. There's a silver (un-aged) option, or Bayou Select, which is aged in American oak casks. They also produce a satsuma-flavoured rum.

Prichard's
Prichard's was founded by Phil Prichard in 1997, which makes it one of the first of the new wave of rum and whisky distilleries in the US. Based out of an old school building in Kelso, Tennessee, Prichard's produce Fine Rum, which is matured for at least three years in American oak casks and Private Stock, which bears no age but is aged for, I would guess, about 10 years.

Privateer
This distillery makes Privateer Rum in two expressions: Silver Dry and True American Rum. Both are based on a six-day fermentation of molasses and brown sugar. The former un-aged and the latter aged in whisky and brandy casks.

Rational Spirits
Like Lost Spirits, with whom Rational have a partnership, this Charlestown distillery is quite progressive. They currently bottle two rums: Cuban Inspired Rum that – in a non-Cuban manner – is distilled in a potstill; and Santeria, a Jamaican-inspired rum that uses lab-grown bacteria to give the effects of a dunder pit.

Richland Distilling Company
Made in Richland, Georgia, Richland Rum produce Single Estate Old Georgia Rum, which is based on cane syrup partly derived from the Vennebroeck Estate. The fermented syrup is distilled in a 1,000-litre (53-US gallon) pot still,

then matured for around three years in American oak casks before bottling.

Skip Rock Distillers
Based in Washington, Skip Rock produce the Belle Rose rum brand made from Louisiana turbinado cane sugar. Belle Rose Light Rum is aged in vintage white wine barrels, Amber Rum spends time in ex-bourbon casks, while the Double Barrel Rum starts in bourbon barrels and finishes in French oak red wine barrels.

St. George
The craftiest of California's craft distilleries makes two *agricole* rums from sugarcane grown in the Imperial Valley of Southern California. The first is a very grassy un-aged expression; the second is matured for four years in French oak.

Wiggly Bridge
This Maine-based distillery uses a homemade small-capacity copper pot still. The barrels they use are small too – hence the name Small Barrel Rum – and they also bottle a white rum.

Wicked Dolphin
Founded in 2012 in Cape Coral, this distillery use 100% Florida-grown sugarcane to produce their copper pot still rums. The spirit is matured in ex-bourbon casks for at least one year.

US VIRGIN ISLANDS
Cruzan
With origins in a sugar mill established on St. Croix during the 1750s, this was renamed the Cruzan Rum Distillery in 1963. It's now owned by Suntory but operated by the Nelthropp family. A pure and simple five-column-still distillate is produced here, which soaks up the flavour of oak casks. The standout

ABOVE The USVI has always been dedicated to alcohol consumption. The capital city Charlotte Amalie was known as Taphus in the 17th century, which is the Danish for "beer hall".

the newer extra-añejo Linaje (lineage). A pot still is also used to produce rum for their flagship 1796 bottling, the product of a "solera warehouse".

product is the Single Barrel, a blend of 5- and 12-year-old rums blended and re-casked in new American oak. It tastes a lot like American bourbon whiskey.

VENEZUELA

Destilerias Unidas

Established in 1959 near La Miel, this distillery is best known for the Diplomático rum brand. It also produces the Cacicque and Pampero brands for Diageo. Rum is made from molasses or cane honey and the quirky still house contains two pot stills, columns and a unique batch still for the complex processes that occur here. Diplomatico's super-premium expressions are among the sweetest rums available.

Santa Teresa

In the state of Aragua, the highly respected Santa Teresa distillery is run by the fifth generation of the Vollmer family. They operate a four-column system to produce core expressions such as Santa Teresa Claro and Gran Reserva, aged for 2–3 years and 2–5 years respectively and

ABOVE 1796 bears almost no resemblance to the rest of the Santa Teresa pack, and if you ask me, that's more to do with the use of pot stills than it is complex maturation systems.

GLOSSARY

Añejo A Spanish term used to mean "aged" or "old", indicating that the spirit has spent time in an oak cask.

Angel's Share A portion of maturing spirit that is lost due to evaporation from the cask.

Blackstrap (molasses) The black viscous left-overs from sugar refining; the base material for most of the big rum brands.

Bourbon cask 180–200 litre (48–53 US gallon) charred American oak cask.

Brix A measurement of sweetness in molasses or cane juice/syrup. A liquid of 30° Brix will consist of three parts sugar to seven parts other materials.

Butt Large 500-litre (132-US gallon) cask traditionally used for storing sherry.

Caramel Non-sweet colour additive used to add the effect of longer maturation and for colour consistency. Not permitted in bourbon and straight whiskey.

Charring Non-penetrative and aggressive flame burning of the internal surface of a cask to liberate flavourful compounds and aid with spirit interaction; barrels may be charred to various degrees.

Chill Filtering Controversial finishing process used for some whiskies wherein the liquid is cooled to below 0°C (32°F) and filtered to remove flavourless residual haze that can be unsightly. Critics believe the process also removes body and flavour.

Cooper Maker and mender of barrels for the wine and spirits industry.

Ester A chemical compound formed by the interaction of an acid and an alcohol. Typically smells fruity and floral.

Ethanol Ethyl alcohol, the main type of alcohol present in fermented and distilled beverages.

First-fill A barrel that is being filled for the first time with malt whisky/Irish whiskey, but has typically already been filled with bourbon or sherry – so actually it is a second fill!

Finishing The practice of taking a mature spirit (generally aged previously in an ex bourbon cask) and ageing it for an additional short period of time in another type of cask. The period of finishing can be anywhere from six months to many years, and it's usually sherry, wine and ex-brandy casks that are used.

Mothballed A distillery that has ceased production, but not been decommissioned (i.e. its equipment remains in place).

Oxidation (In reference to maturation) the process of converting alcohol into aldehydes and acids in the cask, which leads to ester formation.

Pot Still A traditional distillation kettle used to concentrate fermented products into a spirit. Typically pot stills are heated by gas, steam, or direct fire (wood, coal).

Solera From the Spanish word meaning "ground" or "earth". This is a system of cask maturation whereby casks are filled in tiers from top to bottom with the lower tiers being filled from the upper. Spirit is only removed from the bottom tier, hence the name "solera". Each tier is never completely emptied, meaning that some small amount of rum will remain in the system throughout the lifespan of the system, aiding in consistency and sort of doing the job of a blender.

Stave Shaped piece of wood used to construct a cask.

Toasting A process of heating the inside surface of a barrel/cask through radiant or convective heat (rather than direct flames as is the case with "charring").

Vesou Fresh sugarcane juice.

Vieux A French term meaning "old" that is used to signify a rum that has been matured for a period of time.

Viejo A Spanish term meaning "old" that is used to signify a rum that has been matured for a period of time.

Vin (In reference to *rhum agricole*) Fermented cane juice.

Vinasse (In reference to *rhum agricole*) the waste water left over from the distillation of *vesou* (cane wine).

Virgin (In maturation) a new cask that has not held any liquid

Worm tub Traditional manner of converting alcohol vapour into liquid. A "worm" is a coiled pipe that sits in a "tub" of cool water. As the vapour passes through the coil, it condenses into new-make spirit. Worm tubs typically give a heavier, more sulphurous spirit.

INDEX

ABOUT THE AUTHOR

Tristan Stephenson is an award-winning bar operator, bartender, barista, chef, some-time journalist and the bestselling author of The Curious Bartender series of drinks books. In 2009 he was ranked 3rd in the UK Barista Championships. He was then awarded UK bartender of the year in 2012, and in the same year was included in London Evening Standard's annual round up of the 'Top 1000 most influential Londoners'.

After intially launching his career working in various restaurant kitchens in his native Cornwall (on the South West coast of England), in 2007 Tristan was given the opportunity to design cocktails and run bar operations at chef Jamie Oliver's Fifteen. He went on from there to work for the world's biggest premium drinks company, Diageo, and then to co-found Fluid Movement with Thomas Aske (a fellow former drinks industry brand ambassador) in 2009. Their globally renowned drinks consultancy has been the brains behind the drinks programmes at some of the world's top drinking and eating destinations. Fluid Movement then went on to open their own bars in London – Purl, in 2010, and then the highly successful Worship Street Whistling Shop in 2011. (The Whistling Shop was named by Time Out as 'London's Best New Bar' in 2011 and was placed in the 'World's Fifty Best Bars' for three consecutive years.) In 2014 Tristan and Thomas opened their next venue together. Surfside, a family-friendly steak and lobster restaurant on Polzeath beach, this time back in Tristan's native Cornwall. The restaurant was awarded the No. 1 Position in The Sunday Times's newspapers 'Best alfresco dining spots in the UK 2015.' Tristan himself served as head chef there for the first summer and continues to closely manage the food and beverage menu. Surfside has since become a well-established and a popular part of the Cornwall summer and surfing scene.

In 2016 Fluid Movement opened a small hotel with no less than three more London bars, all at the same site in fashionable Shoreditch in the East End of London. The hotel, The Napoleon, was unique in that it had just one bedroom! And the bars (all of which provided room service...) were The Devil's Darling (a classic cocktail bar), Sack (a sherry and tapas bar), and most significantly, Black Rock (a bar dedicated to whisky). Significantly, because Black Rock has won Time Out's 'UK's Best Specialist Bar' for three years consecutively (from 2017–2019). The original intimate basement space has since expanded to also include the first-floor Black Rock Tavern, styled after the izakayas of Japan, and offering whisky highballs, draught beers and a curated collection of malts, bourbons and ryes from around the world. A second Black Rock site opened in Bristol in the Summer of 2019 and further bar openings are planned across the UK.

Tristan's writing debut, The Curious Bartender Volume I: The Artistry & Alchemy of Creating the Perfect Cocktail was published in 2013 and shortlisted for the prestigious André Simon Award for excellence in food and drink writing. His second book, The Curious Bartender: An Odyssey of Malt, Bourbon & Rye Whiskies (from which this book is abridged) hit the bookshelves in 2014. In 2015 he published The Curious Barista's Guide to Coffee (his credentials as a barista as well as a bartender coming into play) and he had, in addition, harvested, processed, roasted and brewed the first cup of UK-grown coffee from the Eden Project in Cornwall. In 2016 his fourth book, in what was by now an established series, The Curious Bartender's Gin Palace, was again shortlisted for the André Simon and took readers on a tour of the most exciting gin distilleries the world has to offer. His fifth book,

The Curious Bartender's Rum Revolution, appeared in 2017 and demonstrated how rum has moved beyond its Caribbean heartlands, with new distilleries appearing in Brazil, Venezuela, Colombia and Guatemala and in very unexpected places, such as Australia, Japan, Mauritius and the Netherlands. His sixth title, The Curious Bartender Volume 2: The New Testament, (an eagerly anticipated follow-up to the original bestselling Curious Bartender Volume 1) was met with great enthusiasm by his worldwide bartending fanbase upon publication in 2018. Once again it featured classic cocktail recipes plus Tristan's own highly imaginative spins and in-depth explanation of classic drinks and modern mixology methods.

Then in 2019 Tristan brought the growing number of American whiskey and bourbon collectors and fans The Curious Bartender's

Whiskey Road Trip. This coast-to-coast tour of the most exciting whiskey distilleries in the US, 'from small-scale craft operations to the behemoths of bourbon', is surely one of Tristan's most impressive and ambitious works to date. Finally, Tristan's other commercial enterprises include his drinks brand Aske-Stephenson (again with business partner Fluid Movement's Thomas Aske) which manufactures and sells pre-bottled cocktails in flavours as diverse as Rhubarb & Custard Negroni, Bramble Garden, Peanut Butter & Jam Old-fashioned, Sesame & Popcorn Daiquiri and Flat White Russian. He has also launched an on-line whisky subscription service, whisky-me.com, offering top-quality single malt whiskies for home delivery. In addition, in March 2017 Tristan joined the supermarket chain Lidl UK as a consultant on their highly-regarded own-brand spirits range.

Tristan travels extensively for work but lives in Cornwall and is husband to Laura and father to two small children. In his very limited spare time he runs, rides a Triumph motorcycle, takes photos, designs websites, bakes stuff, cooks a lot, reads avidly, attempts various DIY tasks beyond his level of ability and collects whiskey and books.

ACKNOWLEDGMENTS

To my family: Laura, Dexter, Robin, Mum, Linda & Rod.

The extended family: Tom & Mona, Craig & Emma, Barrie & Amie, Daryl & Hannah and Jake (thanks for the WN17).

To my rum-mates all over the world: Mike Aikman, Jimmy Barrat, Jacob Briars, Dave Broom, Ian Burrell, Ryan Chetiyawardana, Arnaud Chevalier, Paolo Figueiredo, James Fowler, Simon Ford, Matt Hastings, Peter Holland, Stu McCluskey, Jason Scott, Thomas Soldberg, Tom Walker and Claire & Dan Warner.

To Darren Rook, my one and only travelling buddy who joined me on the no-seatbelt tour of Haiti and who is probably the sole reason that I am not still there.

To those who helped orchestrate or fit in with the various impossibly complex elements of the rum tour: Aurelie Bapte, Daniel Baudin, Shaun Caleb, Gordon Clark, Matt Dakers, Henry Damoiseau, Dan Dove, Benjamin Jones, Alexandre Gabriel, John Georges, Jon Lister, Michael Callwood, Calbert Apollo Francis, José Class, Enrique Comas, Jenny Gardener, Karen Garnik, Yenia Gomez, Phillipa Greaves, Alexander Kong, Pascal Lambert, Ian McLaren, Paul McFadyen Margaret Monplaisir, Alexx Mouzouris, Nestor Ortega, Darrio Prescod, Lynn Valerie Romain, Stephen Rutherford, Michel Sajous, Meimi Sanchez, Chris Seale, Richard Seale, Roberto Serrallés, Don Shillingford, Allen Smith, Miguel Smith, Michael Speakman, Joy Spence, Jordan Telford, Lorena Vasquez, Fritz & Itsel Vaval, Henry Vickrobeck, Jassil Villanueva, Leanne Ware and Simon & Larry Warren.

To all of the hosts that put me up along the way, and in most cases shared a glass of rum or two: Gilles and his old bottle of Dillon, Patricia & Gabriel drinking Ti punch, Sylvain & Marie Anne sleeping in hammocks, Val & Nico on their wonderful boat, Warren & Tracey and their jungle retreat, Tereen, Larry & Terrel in fantastic Grenada, Hannes & Sara for a whirlwind three days in Barbados, Martha for organising everything, Karyn, Cyril for the coconuts, Luis & Amber, Akeem, Lorenzo, and last but not least, Sergio.

Thanks also to Simon & Lori Crompton for a great night out on Grand Cayman. I owe you both a drink.

Other kind and hospitable folk I met along the way: Kenrick, Gideon, Delon… and many, many more whose names escape my memory but of whom the memories do not.

Finally, to the amazing production team at RPS and beyond: Nathan (glutton for punishment), Geoff, Julia, Leslie, Cindy, David, Christina and Trish. And to Addie, Lei and Sari.

Five down… that's gone quickly.

PICTURE CREDITS KEY: al: above left, ar: above right, bl: below left, br: below right